Praise for *The Business of Being*

"*The Business of Being* sets itself apart through engaging stories, actionable steps, and a dash of humor. Deftly closing the gap between business and spirituality, it encourages current or prospective business owners to live in alignment with inner values without compromising integrity. Those who take this book to heart will undergo a powerful transformation in both their personal and business lives."
—**STEPHEN J. HOPSON,** the world's first deaf instrument-rated pilot and author of *Obstacle Illusions: Transforming Adversity into Success*

"When we allow ourselves to show up authentically—be who we are—we're in alignment. *The Business of Being* helps us unlock the power to reach our full potential and thrive."
—**RACHAEL O'MEARA,** transformational leadership and executive coach, sales executive at Google, and author of *Pause: Harnessing the Life-Changing Power of Giving Yourself a Break*

"*The Business of Being* is an important resource that will enable individuals to discover their calling and transform their personal and professional lives."
—**DR. LYNN SCHMIDT,** leadership development expert, executive coach, keynote speaker, and award-winning coauthor of *Shift Into Thrive: Six Strategies for Women to Unlock the Power of Resiliency*

"Laurie Buchanan is a master storyteller. In *The Business of Being*, she expertly weaves the development story of a French restaurant business with the exploration story of personal being. Individuals considering creative business partnerships will gain insights on charting a successful business and collaboration. However, the essence of the book is an imaginative and resource rich guide to hearing and responding to the internal call to one's authentic *raison d'etre*. It offers a pleasurable recipe for stirring our personal being and responding to it."
—**AUDREY B. DENECKE,** Senior Leader Coach and Organizational Change Consultant

"*The Business of Being* is the best silent partner I ever took on."

—**TERRILL WELCH,** gallery owner and author of *Leading Raspberry Jam Visions Women's Way: An Inside Track for Women Leaders*

"This gem of a book is really three books in one: a savvy guide to building a business, an engaging story of a boutique restaurant, and a coaching guide to living an intentional life. Chock full of quotes and stories and examples, *The Business of Being* will help you be the person (and the business) you want to be. And in doing so, she shows you how to change the world, and have fun doing so. Bravo!"

—**RITA SEVER,** author of *Supervision Matters: 100 Bite-Sized Ideas to Transform You and Your Team*

"The book combines a personal guide and business manual with a culinary story . . . lays out a series of plain-sounding but persuasively thoughtful principles organized around the straightforward contention that there really isn't much difference between the two disciplines, asking a deceptively simple question: 'Can implementing business values improve personal lives?' . . . A lucid, step-by-step guide to personal and professional success—with *vichyssoise* mixed in."

—*KIRKUS REVIEWS*

"When I received Laurie Buchanan's new book, *The Business of Being,* I started reading it immediately because I had enjoyed her first book so much. This second effort is not a disappointment! Buchanan has written a straight-to-the-heart book on building a successful business, not only professionally, but in tandem with your personal "business." This book is a smart resource with some recipes thrown in, to live with authenticity and to merge best business practices with your best self. Loved it!"

—**MARIANNE LILE,** author of *Stepmother: A Memoir*

"This book is enlightening, inspiring, and thoroughly enjoyable. Through stories, research, and her own experience and wisdom, Buchanan shows readers how to build a successful and responsible business while at the same time assuring that they live a satisfying and purposeful life. Woven in to illustrate many of her points is the delicious tale of how an eclectic group of friends envisioned and launched a charming French restaurant—from inception, to opening, to sustained success. Buchanan is a teacher/guide who combines business acumen with spiritual awareness and masterful storytelling."

—**DONNA CAMERON,** author of *A Year of Living Kindly: Choices That Will Change Your Life and the World Around You*

"I can say with confidence that whether you're new to business or have been at it awhile, *The Business of Being* will educate, energize, and delight you. Laurie Buchanan knows exactly how to speak to the head and the heart!"

—**CRISTEN IRIS,** editor, writer, book and business coach

"Unlike so many others in the self-help book business, Laurie Buchanan makes no promises that you will 'think and grow rich.' Even though she uses business best practices as teaching moments, the goal is sustainability over wealth, integrity over profit, and the joy of the journey over the destination. Unlike many spiritual writers, she does not denigrate the physical world or the sensory world. In fact, quite the opposite! The business she chooses to use as the example of combining self and business is a restaurant, featuring the most sensory of all cuisines—French. I found myself totally absorbed in the story of how *La Mandarine Bleue* came into existence as an extension of relationships among talented friends whose love of good food and wine, and whose shared values but varied gifts, make a compelling story that illustrates the thesis."

—**SHIRLEY HERSHEY SHOWALTER,** former president of, and professor at, Goshen College, and author of *Blush: A Mennonite Girl Meets a Glittering World*

The Business of Being

The Business of Being

SOUL PURPOSE IN AND

OUT OF THE WORKPLACE

Laurie Buchanan, PhD

SHE WRITES PRESS

Published 2018
Printed in the United States of America
ISBN: 978-1-63152-395-3 pbk
ISBN: 978-1-63152-396-0 ebk
Library of Congress Control Number: 2018935584

For information, address:
She Writes Press
1563 Solano Ave #546
Berkeley, CA 94707

She Writes Press is a division of SparkPoint Studio, LLC.

Interior design by Tabitha Lahr

This book is dedicated to the people in
my personal and professional life
who've closed the gap between what they say
and what they do—who *walk the talk*.
It's an honor to be in your sphere of influence.

Contents

SECTION TEN

SECTION ELEVEN

SECTION TWELVE

Foreword

Being. **"Being" is a powerful word.** Laurie Buchanan defines "being" as internal in nature and reflective. *"Doing"* is external in nature; it is visible and active. I believe as children, being comes more naturally to us. We wander and wonder. Then as we move into adulthood, the ability "to be" gets lost along the way as our careers and busy lives consume us. Doing takes over our lives and being gets sidelined. We lose our ability to reflect and restore.

In the middle of my career, I described myself to a colleague as a hamster on a hamster wheel: spinning round and round, racking up accomplishments, and yet not feeling satisfied. While I couldn't quite put my finger on what was causing my dissatisfaction, it was there, and it continued to grow. Finally, I realized I needed time "to be." I gave myself the gift of a one-year sabbatical. I got rid of all my stuff, moved to Europe for a year, and wrote a book about women, work, and resiliency. During my sabbatical, I relearned what the business of being was all about. I wandered and wondered. I reflected and was restored. Now I make sure my life includes both doing and being.

The Business of Being enables readers to learn how to marry doing and being by finding a vocation: a calling. Laurie describes a vocation as something that brings deep fulfillment and excites us. It may be a career or something outside a career. Through time-tested theories, real-life examples, and an engaging story, *The Business of Being* provides the twelve ingredients of a business plan. When these ingredients are mixed together they create the perfect recipe for personal and professional transformation.

In this book, Laurie provides readers with the tools and techniques necessary to implement each element of the business plan and personalize it to meet their needs. There are tips to help individuals navigate the journey. Quotes and real-life examples do an excellent job of bringing the concepts to life. The story of *La Mandarine Bleue* is a wonderful depiction of how nine individuals used the twelve steps of the business plan to find their vocation and undergo a transformation. And the *pièces de résistance* is the French recipes. *Mangez bien!*

The Business of Being is an important resource that will enable individuals to discover their calling and transform their personal and professional lives.

—Dr. LYNN SCHMIDT, leadership development expert, executive coach, keynote speaker, and award-winning coauthor of *Shift Into Thrive: Six Strategies for Women to Unlock the Power of Resiliency*

Preface

"Everyone has his own specific vocation or mission in life; everyone must carry out a concrete assignment that demands fulfillment. Therein he cannot be replaced, nor can his life be repeated, thus, everyone's task is unique as his specific opportunity to implement it."

—VIKTOR FRANKL, neurologist, psychiatrist,
Holocaust survivor, and author

I ran away from home—sunny southern California to the overcast Pacific Northwest—when I was fifteen. Lying about my age, I applied at one of those everything-under-one-roof superstores and got a job. Over the next five years, I worked my way from entry-level cashier to management.

During that five-year timeframe, I had occasion to attend corporate meetings at the company headquarters in Portland. On a few of those visits I had the opportunity to meet the founder, the man responsible for implementing the company's governing beliefs:

- Customers are essential, for without them we'd have no business.
- Customers shop most where they believe their needs and wants will be satisfied best.

○ Satisfactory profits are essential, without profits our business can neither grow nor meet the needs and wants of our customers, employees, suppliers, shareholders, or the community.

○ Skilled, capable, and dedicated employees are essential, for the overall success of our business is determined by the combined ideas, work, and effort of all the company's employees.

Based on these beliefs, we commit to:

○ Serving customers so well that after shopping with us they are satisfied and will want to shop with us again.

○ Operating our business efficiently and effectively, so we earn a satisfactory profit today and in the future.

○ Providing an environment that encourages employees to develop their abilities, use their full potential, and share ideas that further the success of the business, so they gain a sense of pride in their accomplishments and confidence in their capabilities.

○ We believe that by following this philosophy, we will satisfy customers and earn their patronage, provide for the profitable growth of our company, and enrich the lives of the company's employees and their families.[1]

I hadn't thought about that employment experience in decades until my husband and I relocated from twenty-three years in the greater Chicagoland area to the temperate climate of southwestern Idaho and I saw one of the stores. I pulled into the parking lot, entered the doors, and a flood of good memories rushed in. As a businesswoman, I wondered:

Does this superstore—that has since been bought by a megastore but operates under the same name—still practice its fundamental governing beliefs? Have the original principles been expanded? Have they been compromised?

But more important, as a transformational life coach I wanted to answer this question, "Can implementing business values improve personal lives?"

To get the answers, I applied for a job. During the interview process, I explained the purpose of my application for employment—to get back in the trenches so I could answer those questions honestly and write a book from a present-day perspective that would benefit my clients.

As a holistic health practitioner, I was an ideal fit for a position in their nutrition center. Thus began my two-year, behind-the-scenes investigative look at what moves the current-day business forward—and what holds it back.

Not new to the business world, this superstore experience was on the heels of twenty-five years in business: eleven in the corporate world (recruiting and communication) and fourteen in private practice.

This book is the culmination of research, personal experience, and hundreds of conversations with employees at every level, customers, and clients.

Job, Career, and Vocation—The Differences

The Business of Being looks at the world of business as it relates to our personal lives. And because companies are comprised of individuals, let's take a moment to clarify the differences between job, career, and vocation.

A *job* is something that's limited in duration. It's a monetary stopgap until we find something long-term: a career. In their book, *Designing Your Life*, authors Bill Burnett and Dave Evans say, "In America, two-thirds of workers are unhappy with their jobs. And fifteen percent actually hate their work."

A *career* can span decades, and it generates income. Often people include their careers when making introductions because our career is a large part of who we are. Another startling statistic in *Designing Your Life* is "In the United States, only twenty-seven percent of college grads end up in a career related to their majors."

A *vocation* is a calling. The word is a derivative of the Latin *vocare*, or voice (God's voice). It's something that brings deep fulfillment, is meaningful, joyful, and excites us; it might even have a positive social impact. It can be our career, or it can be separate. It can be commercially viable but not necessarily.

In his book *Wishful Thinking: A Seeker's ABC*, author Frederick Buechner says, "The place God calls you is the place where your deep gladness and the world's deep hunger meet." Vocation occupies the place where the crosshairs intersect.

One of my colleagues is researching the connection between vocation and aging. In her *Forbes* article, "A Better Way to Say 'I'm Retired,'" author and former president of, and professor at, Goshen College, Shirley Hershey Showalter wrote, "The coolest thing about a vocation is that it can be practiced anywhere. You don't need a job. It helps if you have had a career related to your vocation, but only because a career gives you lots of opportunity to practice."

If you ask Shirley, "What do you do?" she answers, "Jubilee." When prompted to elaborate, she explains, "Latin Americans have no such word for the concept of 'retirement.' I didn't know this. Instead, they use the word *jubilación* for the post-career stage of life."

She expands: "*Jubilación* means jubilation in English. The root word is jubilee. If you substitute *jubilation* for retirement, you can call your work in the elder stages 'jubilee.' From there, it is easy to get to the alliterative phrase 'my job is jubilee.'"[2]

A perfect fit, the Merriam-Webster dictionary defines jubilee as "a season of celebration."[3]

Do Be Do Be Do. . .

I'm often asked for my thoughts about the difference between *doing* and *being* and which one I feel is more important.

One of the byproducts of today's fast-paced culture is *busyness*. With our amazing technology, we're efficient, productive, and more inclined than ever to use our time to accomplish.

In color therapy, *doing* is associated with yellow. Visible and active, doing is external in nature. Doing stirs things up. It's in the act of doing that we serve others.

In color therapy, *being* is associated with violet. Invisible and passive, being is internal in nature. Being is reflective. When we listen in the quietness of being, we learn what to do.

"Don't just do something—sit there!"

—SYLVIA BOORSTEIN, psychotherapist, co-founding
teacher at Spirit Rock Meditation Center, and author

Interestingly, yellow and violet reside directly across from each other on the color wheel. In nature, a beautiful depiction of this balance can be seen in ametrine, a semiprecious stone that's a natural blend of amethyst (violet/purple) and citrine (yellow/gold).

In our everyday lives, the balance between doing and being is expressed as:

○ Engagement and solitude
○ Serving and abiding
○ Real life and reflective life
○ Application and restoration
○ Work and rest

Weaving a balanced combination of both threads—doing and being—into our life's tapestry is ideal; they're both important. A balanced life of doing and being nourishes both practice and perspective.

"People who can make an explicit connection between their work and something socially meaningful to them are more likely to find satisfaction, and are better able to adapt to the inevitable stresses and compromises that come with working in the world."

—MARTIN SELIGMAN, psychologist, educator,
and author

Introduction

"All you need is the plan, the road map, and the courage to press on to your destination."

—**EARL NIGHTINGALE,** radio personality, speaker, and author

This book isn't about being in business; it's about the business of being. But when you stop to think about it, each of us is like a small business.

Successful business owners implement strategies that improve their prospects for success. Similarly, as human beings, it serves us well to implement guiding principles that inspire us to live our purpose and reach our **goals**.

By merging the language of business with self-help, this book stakes out new cross-marketing territory, bridging the gap between career and spirituality. It shows how to use everyday business practices and strategies to manage personal growth and success.

From a business plan and metrics to mission and goals, and with everything between—investors, clients and customers, **marketing** strategies, and goodwill development—*The Business of Being* clearly maps how to create personal transformation at the intersection of business and spirituality; how to enhance "profitability"—body, mind, and spirit.

La Mandarine Bleue

The chapters in this book are designed like a decadent chocolate sandwich cookie.

The lightly sweet wafer on one side reviews a single business plan element.

The delicious wafer on the other side is its counterpart in our personal lives and shows how the concept can be used to make *being* even better.

The sinfully rich ganache filling between is the story of *La Mandarine Bleue*, a French restaurant that shows from start to finish—*hors d'oeuvres* to *café*—how the elements (ingredients of a business plan) are dished up and served to perfection in real life.

Using *La Mandarine Bleue* and its founders as examples, *The Business of Being* walks readers through twelve elements of a business plan via a classic French twelve-course meal. It walks through the steps its founders took and what they opted to do at each stage to establish their restaurant. And each section includes a *délicieux* recipe.

Taking creative license to protect their identities, the story of *La Mandarine Bleue* is the business story you'll find woven throughout the pages of this book.

A bientôt—cheers!

"Be a fearless cook! Try out new ideas and new recipes, but always buy the freshest and finest ingredients, whatever they may be. Furnish your kitchen with the most solid and workmanlike equipment you can find. Keep your knives ever sharp and—*toujours bon appétit!*"

—JULIA CHILD, chef, television personality, and author

SECTION ONE

Business Plan

La Mandarine Bleue

Course One—*Hors d'oeuvres*

Put Your Stake in the Ground

Business Plan

"Everything I do, and everything Pixar does is based on a simple rule: Quality is the best business plan, period."

—**JOHN LASSETER,** animator, Chief Creative Officer of Pixar Animation Studios, Principal Creative Advisor for Walt Disney Imagineering, and film director

Personal or business, planning is about results.

Survival in the business world is dependent upon a business plan—a powerful declaration of goals and intentions, a written summary of what we aim to accomplish and an overview of how we intend to organize our resources to attain these goals.

Whether financial assistance is obtained to start a business or not, it's imperative to have a comprehensive business plan. Not static, a business plan is a living document that's regularly monitored, evaluated, and revised. It's comprised of several elements:

- ○ Mission and Vision
- ○ **Core Values**
- ○ Goals and Objectives
- ○ **Market Segmentation** and **Targeting**
- ○ Competitive Environment
- ○ **Definition of Offering**

○ **Market** Positioning and Strategy
○ Marketing and Selling Model
○ Product Launch
○ Operations and Organization
○ Financial Analysis

A business plan is a roadmap for success in business. It typically projects three to five years out and details the route a company intends to take to increase revenues. It's also a management tool that helps you evaluate progress and points to areas that need attention.

An interactive document, a business plan provides clarity, sets the tone for the business, and can serve as a **benchmarking** tool. It also fosters alignment. Doreen Bloch of Poshly Inc. says, "Writing a business plan is an ideal way to make sure that everyone on your team is aligned with the current and future plans for the business."[1]

A well-written business plan ensures flow, which is the opposite of stagnation—the death knell of business.

One of the most frightening things a writer can encounter is writer's block—the opposite of flow. Sitting down to create an article or essay, we fully expect original thoughts and creative ideas to flow down from our brain, through our arms, out our fingertips, and onto the keyboard. If this doesn't happen, the result can be white-knuckled fear and paralysis.

This is true in many areas of life:

○ Whether it's family or friends, we expect flow in our daily encounters with other people.
○ Whether it's with coworkers or the task at hand, we expect flow in the workplace—and flow in our commute to get there and back again.
○ Whether it's at the bank, the post office, or making travel arrangements, we expect flow when conducting business transactions.

You've heard the saying "in the zone." Personally or professionally, it's a good place to be—it's flow. It happens when what we're doing is going well; it feels effortless, and even exciting. We become so immersed in the moment that we lose track of time; it seems to stand still.

An athlete is in the flow when they're performing at their best. A musician is in the flow when they're creating beautiful music. A dancer is in the flow when their movements are flawless. A business is in the flow when it is acting out its **mission statement**, when **objectives** are being met and goals achieved.

Flow is dynamic: moving and changing. The image that comes to mind when I think of flow is running water—like a river—and being carried along in a kayak or a canoe. It's immensely enjoyable, practically effortless, yet full of energy. When we encounter anything other than flow, something's amiss. It indicates blockage or even stagnation.

A healthy business plan exhibits vim, vigor, and vitality—characteristics of flow. The individual components work in harmony causing everything to flow in the same direction. Sometimes the flow pushes against obstacles along the way. In so doing, new behaviors, patterns, or limits emerge, giving birth to inspiration—the driving force behind every creative person and great organization.

> "If it really was a no-brainer to make it on your own in business, there'd be millions of no-brained, harebrained, and otherwise dubiously brained individuals quitting their day jobs and hanging out their own shingles. Nobody would be left to round out the workforce and execute the business plan."
>
> —**BILL RANCIC,** American entrepreneur

La Mandarine Bleue

"Don't aspire to make a living, aspire to make a difference."

—**CRISTETA COMERFORD,** the first female ever to be
selected as the White House Executive Chef

When my husband and I moved to Boise from the greater
Chicagoland area, we were amazed to discover that Boise, Idaho, has a
food scene that rivals many larger cities. From drinks to desserts, Boise
has it covered.

No matter the geographic location, **foodies** tend to congregate.
Such was the case with a particular group of friends, four couples and a
single woman, who met in the Basque District, became fast friends, and
have since become successful business partners: owners of *La Mandarine
Bleue,* a French restaurant.

Ranging in age from early fifties to midseventies, they live within
five miles of each other. There are nine historic preservation districts in
Boise: East End, North End, Hays Street, Warm Springs Avenue, Harrison
Boulevard, Hyde Park, Old Boise, South Eighth Street, and Spaulding.

Sally is a successful marketing executive who has lived in Hyde
Park for eight years. In a city neighborhood, eight years would have
earned her dinosaur status, but small towns operate under an altered
sense of time, which drops her firmly into the midrange category. Not
quite new, yet not a long-time resident.

Hyde Park is described as "a thriving commercial district from the turn of the century, providing two barbers, a pharmacy, meat market, bicycle shop, hotel, shoe shop, milliner, dyer, dairy, post office, bakery, plumber, and lumber yard. Streetcar service supported the district, connecting it to the surrounding neighborhood and downtown."[2]

Long-time residents of Hyde Park, Larry and his younger partner Dwayne occupy a house two blocks from Sally. They moved there ages ago after a blow from Larry's San Francisco boss put him into early retirement from his upper-management career in the manufacturing industry. Although he'd received the news of his dismissal only a few months before his sixtieth birthday Larry felt short-changed and poured himself into everything French, from learning the language to making its cuisine.

Writing under the pseudonym Scarlett (like Cher, no last name required), Dwayne is a prolific writer who—much to his publisher's delight—produces award-winning novels that fly off bookstore shelves as if winged.

Larry and Dwayne entertain on a regular basis, and invitations to their impromptu get-togethers are coveted.

Trust-fund babies Sheila and Peter live in a mansion, rebuilt with an eye on historic authenticity, in the Warm Springs Avenue historic district. Dedicated to making the world a better place, they're politically active doing what they can to encourage others to vote, and they volunteer for causes they care deeply about.

And though he's not a *sommelier*, Peter's knowledge of, and enthusiasm for, wine borders on that of an expert. He loves to explain that wine isn't a simple beverage. It's a discovery. The aroma and origin are all a part of a grand story just waiting to be told.

Sheila's passion is literacy. A dedicated volunteer at the Idaho Commission for Libraries, she shares their goal of "getting books into the hands of youth unlikely to have many in their homes and those who often have challenges getting to library programs."[3] She's also a proud steward of a Little Free Library box that she checks every day.

The Boise City website says that "the homes on Warm Springs Avenue are distinctive, grand, and designed in diverse architectural styles. The combination of stately homes and medians makes this area one of Boise's most historically significant local districts as well as one of the most unique in the western states."[4]

Moroccan-born, Yousef and Amina are partners in love and work. Artists, they're known for their environmental works many of which are large-scale installations constructed in outdoor settings. And though their work is high-profile, they maintain a low-profile lifestyle in the North End where they live in a small bungalow.

The North End is described as "developed as a working and middle-class neighborhood, hence the preponderance of modest bungalows; but the area is also unique for the mixture of housing stock that can be found there."[5]

An adjunct professor at Boise State University—*go Broncos!*—Southern California transplant Zoe teaches advanced courses in math. Weather permitting, she rides her bicycle to school. Never without a camera, she's a multi-time recipient of the Behind the Lens award.

Fifteen years her senior is Bill, a retired financial advisor who comes from a wealthy family but doesn't rest on old-money laurels. Active in the community, he's a volunteer on the supportive services team at the Interfaith Sanctuary, a shelter for men, women, and families with children. In this capacity, he helps people successfully transition out of homelessness. Zoe and Bill live on Harrison Boulevard.

On the Boise City website we read that "as Boise boomed in the first decades of the 20th Century, many of the city's most prominent citizens built their homes on Harrison Boulevard, resulting in a superb collection of architectural styles. With the addition of the median parkway and street lights in 1916, the City Engineer called it a 'model road.' This unique combination of stately homes and medians makes Harrison Boulevard one of Boise's most historic and beautiful neighborhoods."[6]

With each having an 11.11 percent say (although Sally's is 11.12 percent because it was her idea), they agreed that a risk becomes palatable when divided equally between nine bright, tenacious, financially able, business savvy people.

Course One—*Hors d'oeuvres*

Pronounced "or-dervs," this is the appetizer course. Small-portioned dishes served hot or cold before a meal, *hors d'oeuvres* may be served prior to seating, or at the table.

....

Sainte-Maure, Basil, and Fresh Herb Terrine
Serves 8-10

Ingredients
    7 tablespoons slightly salted butter, softened
    ½ shallot, finely chopped
    4 fresh chives, finely chopped
    1 tablespoon walnut oil
    ½ teaspoon coarsely ground black pepper
    1 fresh Sainte-Maure or other goats' cheese
    4 fresh basil leaves
    Sea salt

Preparation
Mix the butter, shallot, chives, walnut oil, and pepper
in a bowl. Cut the cheese into four thick slices. Divide

the shallot, butter, and basil leaves among the slices and reassemble the cheese. Sprinkle with sea salt.

Pairing Note
Enjoy this course with Condrieu, a white wine from the Côtes du Rhône region of France.

Put Your Stake in the Ground

"The purpose of life is a life of purpose."

—**ROBERT BYRNE**, author

A personal business plan is a powerful motivational tool for staying on track and rejuvenating your life. Before we get down to the nitty-gritty of determining your purpose, mission, path, passion, and philosophy, work through the following questions to whet your appetite and get your mental juices flowing. Your answers are the personal counterpart to the business plan element located on the right-hand side of the question:

1. Where am I going?—mission and vision
2. What have I got to offer?—product or service
3. Who do I influence?—clients in the marketplace
4. How much time and effort am I willing to invest?—calculating the cost, financial analysis
5. Where am I now? Where do I want to be?—forecasting growth
6. What's at stake?—risk analysis
7. What are my personal standards?—ethics; not just what's legal, but what's right

8. What is my personal definition of success? By what measure will I know I'm successful?—the bottom line

9. What actions do I need to take to ensure success?—the overall plan

In Dan Buettner's TED talk on "How to Live to 100+," there are some surprising conclusions about the factors that create a long and healthy life. One of the most significant is *ikigai*. According to the Japanese, everyone has an ikigai: "a reason for being." Finding it requires a deep and often lengthy search of self, but taking internal inventory is well worth the effort because it leads to personal fulfillment and satisfaction. As shown below, ikigai lies at the center of interconnecting circles:[7]

For a moment, think of yourself as a business. In our personal lives, determining our purpose is the counterpart to formulating a business plan in the business arena. To accomplish this, you must answer the question, *Why am I here?*

Not your geographic location but your life purpose. Knowing why we're here provides us with the most concrete and basic thing we can know about ourselves—that there's a particular reason for each of us being here.

Women, especially, have trouble answering this question. As mothers, workers, homemakers, artists, social networkers, lovers, chauffeurs, spiritual guides, etc., our purpose can get buried—lost—sometimes.

The bad news is, if you're waiting to *find* your life purpose, you can stop looking now because you're never going to find it.

The good news is, you don't find your purpose. You *determine* it. It's a choice, a conscious decision that you make. It's a stake you put in the ground.

Answer the following questions:

1. *What is my mission?* Your mission is the natural outcome of authentically living your purpose.
2. *What is my path?* Your path is the means by which you accomplish your purpose.
3. *What is my passion?* Your passion is the drive behind your purpose: the force, the enthusiasm. It's the internal *oomph* you apply to a person, place, thing, or experience—a tremendous mental and emotional investment.
4. *What is my philosophy?* Your philosophy is the precept by which you live.

If you're struggling to answer these questions, perhaps reading my answers will provide seed thoughts to get you started. As you'll see, the answers can be short and simple. Notice I don't say, "I hope to," "Maybe," or "I wish." Like Captain Jean-Luc Picard on the Starship USS Enterprise—*"Make it so!"*

Purpose—I am a mindful agent of heart-based change—body, mind, and spirit.

My purpose isn't bound by geographic location; it's totally portable and can be accomplished from any location. Additionally, I can be a mindful agent of heart-based change in any occupation: hair stylist, landscaper, astronaut, accountant, dentist, mechanic, corporate executive. There are no limits.

It's my opinion that knowing one's life purpose—and living it—is vital for dynamic participation in the world and experiencing joy.

Mission—I affect heart-based change.

Remember, our mission is the natural outcome when we live our purpose authentically.

Path—I practice excellence.

I choose to associate with people, places, things, events, and opportunities that are positive, uplifting, constructive, and healing.

Passion—I am fueled by compassion.

It's been said that "Love is an act of kindness and compassion is its companion." If love is an act of kindness then grace is divinity in action.

Beverly Engel, LMFT, author of the article "What Is Compassion and How Can It Improve My Life?" in *Psychology Today* defines compassion as "the ability to understand the emotional state of another person or oneself. Often confused with empathy, compassion has the added element of having a desire to alleviate or reduce the suffering of another."[8]

The next time we see a person and think "There but for the grace of God go I," we have the opportunity to put our divinity into action and be the immediate presence of spirit for that individual; give them a smile, a word of encouragement, or lend them a helping hand.

Philosophy—Whatever you are not changing, you are choosing.

Are you weighed down by an overpacked schedule or a demanding job you don't enjoy? Is carrying unhealthy pounds sapping your energy? Do you fail to keep your promises? Do you bite your fingernails? Do you tell falsehoods? Are you still smoking?

In a conversation with my friend and senior leadership coach Audrey Denecke, she observed, "And even though some circumstances in our life seem unchangeable, what we can change is our attitude toward the situation, circumstance. Sometimes it is our attitude that brings the pain in."

A Personal Approach

I'm inspired by reading the personal philosophies of people who make a positive difference in the world.

Jon Mertz is the founder of the Thin Difference Community and author of *Activate Leadership: Aspen Truths to Empower* **Millennial** *Leaders*. His personal philosophy is, "Live simply. Lead with spirit. Always try to do the right things right. Take time to re-soul."[9]

Oprah Winfrey is an American media proprietor, talk show host, actress, producer, and philanthropist. She says, "My Philosophy is that not only are you responsible for your life, but doing the best at this moment puts you in the best place for the next moment."[10]

Apolo Ohno is a retired short track speed skating competitor and eight-time medalist in the Winter Olympics. His philosophy is, "It is not up to me whether I win or lose. Ultimately, this might not be my day. And it is that philosophy towards sports, something that I really truly live by. I am emotional. I want to win. I am hungry. I am a competitor. I have that fire. But deep down, I truly enjoy the art of competing so much more than the result."[11]

When we determine our purpose, we put our stake in the ground. A stake is something that marks out territory and boundaries. The word "boundary" is defined as "something that indicates or fixes a limit or extent."[12] Boundaries can be physical or emotional and can be applied to many different areas of our lives. Some examples include relationships (platonic and intimate), environments, financial, social, exercise, children, workplace, home, food, and recovery—such as 12-step programs.

It's my perspective that establishing and maintaining boundaries are two different things.

Establishing a boundary is defining it and setting it in place.

Maintaining a boundary is checking it often to sustain it, to ensure that it holds.

Somewhat like the beds in *Goldilocks and the Three Bears*, boundaries can be too hard, too soft, or just right. Using personal relationships to illustrate the point, "just right" boundaries are firm yet flexible, with each person in the relationship giving and receiving support, respecting each other's feelings, needs, opinions, and rights.

In a relationship with healthy boundaries, each person is responsible for their happiness. Likewise, they give the other person the gift of being responsible for their personal happiness. Healthy boundaries grow and change; they're flexible. They can be lowered to enhance intimacy or raised to promote safety.

The characteristics of healthy boundaries include self-respect; non-tolerance of abuse or disrespect; responsibility for exploring and nurturing personal potential; two-way communication of wants, needs, and feelings; expectations of reciprocity; and sharing responsibility and power.

Just as we expect others to value our boundaries, it's equally important for us to respect the boundaries of others. Creating healthy boundaries is a process that takes time and practice. When a boundary is tested—and it will be—stand firm; sometimes this means removing people, places, and things that manipulate, abuse, or try to control you.

"Daring to set boundaries is about having the courage to love ourselves, even when we risk disappointing others."

— BRENÉ BROWN, scholar, public speaker, and author

SECTION TWO

Mission and Vision

"A mission statement is not something you write overnight.
. . . But fundamentally, your mission statement becomes
your constitution, the solid expression of your vision and
values. It becomes the criterion by which you measure
everything else in your life."

—**STEPHEN COVEY**, educator, author, businessman,
and keynote speaker

When companies and business people have clearly defined
mission and **vision statements**—declarations about what a company
stands for, statements of intent that direct the actions of the company—
client engagement is strong and retention high.

Eric Jacobson, a former executive who writes about management
and leadership says, "Mission statements become the deeply ingrained
principle and fabric that guide employee behavior and company decisions and actions—the behaviors the company and employees expect
of themselves." He goes on to say, "Without a statement, the company
will lack soul."[1]

There are many companies—large and small—that don't distinguish between mission and vision statements; they use the terms
interchangeably. Regardless, they're both catalysts for action.

Simply put, the difference between a mission and vision statement is this:

○ A company's *mission* statement declares what the organization does. It builds confidence and represents their daily best.

○ A company's *vision* statement creates momentum and represents their future best—a result of doing their daily best.

Nike's combined mission/vision statement is, "To bring inspiration and innovation to every athlete in the world."[2]

Krispy Kreme and Sounds True are companies that have two separate statements.

Krispy Kreme's mission statement is, "To touch and enhance lives through the joy that is Krispy Kreme."

Their vision statement is, "To be the worldwide leader in sharing delicious tastes and creating joyful memories."[3]

Sounds True's mission statement is, "Sounds True exists to inspire, support, and serve personal transformation and spiritual awakening."

Their vision statement is, "The mission of Sounds True is to find teachers and artists who serve as a gateway to spiritual awakening and to produce, publish, and distribute their work with beauty, intelligence, and integrity. We treat our authors, vendors, and partners in the same way we would want to be treated. We work flexibly and efficiently together to create a cooperative, loving environment that honors respectful authenticity and individual growth. We maintain a healthy level of profitability so that we are an independent and sustainable employee-owned organization."[4]

Here are three examples of companies that use stand-alone vision statements:

Disney—"To make people happy."[5]

Ford—"People working together as a lean, global enterprise to make people's lives better through automotive and mobility leadership."[6]

Avon—"To be the company that best understands and satisfies the product, service, and self-fulfillment needs of women—globally."[7]

When I was in the corporate world, I worked at Aon Hewitt, one of the world's leading HR consulting and outsourcing companies. In **human resources**, we were able to entice potential recruits by leveraging our company's mission/vision statement. Straightforward and ambitious, it was appealing. More important, it was—and still is—true: "To make the world a better place to work."[8]

As you've seen, a mission/vision statement doesn't have to be lengthy or complicated. Here are a few more examples from high-profile companies that many of us are familiar with:

Make-A-Wish Foundation—"We grant the wishes of children with life-threatening medical conditions to enrich the human experience with hope, strength, and joy."[9]

Starbucks—"To inspire and nurture the human spirit—one person, one cup, and one neighborhood at a time."[10]

Ben & Jerry's—"Our product mission drives us to make fantastic ice cream—for its own sake. Our economic mission asks us to manage our company for sustainable financial growth. Our social mission compels us to use our company in innovative ways to make the world a better place."[11]

Whole Foods Market—"At Whole Foods Market®, 'healthy' means a whole lot more. It goes beyond good for you, to also encompass the greater good. Whether you're hungry for better, or simply food-curious, we offer a place for you to shop where value is inseparable from values."[12]

Ninety-Nines—"The Ninety-Nines is the international organization of women pilots that promotes advancement of aviation through education, scholarships, and mutual support while honoring our unique history and sharing our passion for flight."[13]

Apple—One of the most famous mission statements was Steve Jobs' 2011 statement that Apple's DNA was about "technology married with liberal arts, married with the humanities, that yields us the results that make our heart sing."[14]

Tim Cook, Jobs' successor, declares, "At Apple, we believe technology should lift humanity and enrich people's lives in all the ways people want to experience it."[15]

Microsoft—"We believe in what people make possible. Our mission is to empower every person and every organization on the planet to achieve more."[16]

Tuesdays With Laurie—Not just for shareholders, clients/customers also benefit from well-crafted mission statements. My business mission statement—"To be a positive, uplifting, constructive, and healing influence in the lives of those I touch."[17]

Volkswagen—"At Volkswagen, it is our mission to build long-term strategic partnerships with our customers. To assist them in making the right choices for their business needs, by minimizing fleet costs and providing world-class customer service."[18]

AirBnB—"Fighting discrimination and creating a world where anyone can belong anywhere."[19]

Facebook—"To give people the power to share and make the world more open and connected. People use Facebook to stay connected with friends and family, to discover what's going on in the world, and to share and express what matters to them."[20]

It's important to note that not all companies have a mission/vision statement. Some find them restrictive. Tara Darrow, a spokesperson for Nordstrom, says, "We think that a mission statement can limit our people from seeing the business through the eyes of the customer."[21] But the majority of the companies on the 100 Best Companies to Work For list have a mission/vision statement that reflects what the company stands for and the employees are willing to work by.

In 2016, the top ten companies of those listed included Alphabet (née Google), Acuity, The Boston Consulting Group, Wegmans Food Markets, Quicken Loans, Robert W. Baird, Kimley-Horn and Associates, SAS Institute, Camden Property Trust, and Edward Jones.

Let's take a look at number one—Google. According to *Fortune*, "Google has been on the list for ten years with this [2016] being its seventh time at No. 1, thanks to sparking the imagination of its talented and highly compensated workers, and by adding perks to an already dizzying array of freebies. Last year it enhanced health care coverage by offering virtual doctor visits, second-opinion services, and breast-cancer screenings at headquarters. One Googler explained, 'The company culture truly makes workers feel they're valued and respected as a human being, not as a cog in a machine. The perks are phenomenal. From three prepared organic meals a day to unlimited snacks, artisan coffee and tea, to free personal-fitness classes, health clinics, on-site oil changes, haircuts, spa truck, bike-repair truck, nap pods, free on-site laundry rooms, and subsidized wash and fold. The list is endless.'"[22]

"Activity does not always equal progress. Vision without operational excellence just becomes a dream. Great enterprises marry a huge sense of purpose with amazing operational excellence."

—**DEEP NISHAR,** product strategist, investor, and
entrepreneur

La Mandarine Bleue

"Very simply, I pour my heart and soul into the dishes I create and enjoy relaying my love for food to other people."

—**SUZETTE GRESHAM,** executive chef and restauranteur

After much excitement and discussion, the friends decided that the only possible negative to opening a restaurant would be limited to no downtime for each of them, at least in the foreseeable future. They felt it would be manageable for a band of friends and besides, they planned to hire others to help.

Their first meeting was at Sheila and Peter's beautiful home on historic Warm Springs Avenue. An intercom system at the iron-gated entrance allows for quick entry into a semi-circular stonework driveway that could host a convoy. As the heavy oak door opened, they heard Sheila's cheerful invitation, "Welcome everyone, please come in." Barefoot, she and Peter enjoy whole-house geothermal radiant heat flooring. Pointing to a brushed steel shoe rack by the door, Sheila invited their guests to do the same.

On their way to the kitchen, they passed an antique secretary desk in the foyer where one of America's founding fathers sat to edit his biography. Though remodeled, their mansion (circa 1865) exudes authenticity and style.

In the massive kitchen is the original brick oven in a wall that's also home to a double Viking oven. Their kitchen could be a showroom for state-of-the-art, energy-efficient, stainless steel appliances, their perfection highlighted by the natural lighting from expansive windows that offer a stunning view of Boise's foothills.

Peter warmly invited everyone to "belly up to the bar," a huge marble island in the center of the room, so huge they laughingly call it a continent instead of an island. It's surrounded by eight bar stools, four on each side with workstations at each end, covered in supple, sienna-toned leather upholstery. The classic gunmetal steel frames were inspired by French modernist Jean Prouvé.

While everyone took a seat and got comfortable, Peter retrieved wineglasses from a slatted stemware ceiling rack. Before he'd even finished pouring the wine, they'd decided without preamble that their restaurant would serve French cuisine. "Well that was easy," Larry and Dwayne said in unison, and they all laughed.

Over crispy sweet potato goat cheese puffs and a paired-to-perfection Syrah, they determined that Larry would oversee the menu and food preparation. Peter would supervise everything wine, including the stemware. Sally and Zoe would handle **advertising**, marketing, and public relations. Bill would head up business affairs and manage the finances. Yousef and Amina would be in charge of ambiance, including the decor, music, lighting, tableware, etcetera, and once done with those tasks, assist in the kitchen, dining room, or wherever most needed. Sheila and Dwayne would run front of house including reservations, share the task of *maître d'*, and oversee the wait staff.

To get things rolling, they needed a name for their restaurant and to find the perfect location. This would be done as a group. Over a second helping of Sheila's delicious appetizer, Dwayne's eyes fixed on the island's centerpiece—a tall, blown-glass, cobalt-blue bowl flared at the top and filled with tangerines. The light from the pendant fixtures was striking the bowl at an interesting angle that turned the tangerines blue. "I've got the perfect name," he exclaimed smacking his hand on the marble top with excitement. Pointing to the centerpiece, he said, "*La Mandarine Bleue*—the blue tangerine." Smiles spread on the faces all around. Without exception, everyone loved it, and they raised their glasses to the name. *À La Mandarine Bleue. A bientôt!*

With that task completed, Bill suggested they work on a company statement, reminding them that a *mission* statement declares what an organization does; it builds confidence and represents their daily best. And a *vision* statement creates momentum and represents their future best—a result of doing their daily best.

Peter handed out paper and pencils while Zoe helped Sheila put on coffee and gather cups. The enticing aroma from the French press was a delicious accompaniment to the tray of flaky croissants Sheila had baked early that morning. Peter took a jar from the cupboard and popped it open letting the *framboise* fragrance escape and started thickly spreading the raspberry jam on his croissant. No one hesitated to follow suit.

After input from each person, and much addition, deletion, and debate, the owners of *La Mandarine Bleue* created a combined statement that accurately represented both their mission and vision:

> "*La Mandarine Bleue* is committed to an authentic French kitchen, cuisine, and wine. To satisfy parties of every size, our menu includes communal dishes as well as individual choices.
>
> Our dedication to service is exacting, yet our warm approach is welcoming and relaxed in a friendly, vibrant atmosphere.
>
> We do this by consistently providing customers with timely, unintrusive service, demonstrating efficiency, knowledge, professionalism, and integrity in our work.
>
> To ensure fresh, satisfying meals, our seasonally-driven menu is sourced locally whenever possible. Dining at *La Mandarine Bleue* isn't simply a meal; it's an experience."

Everyone agreed that they'd had a productive evening and decided the next step was to find the perfect location—somewhere in the Old Boise Historic District or Central Downtown area in a medium-sized building, preferably one that had been a restaurant in a previous incarnation. Sally, Larry, and Bill were tapped to spearhead that initiative.

In the meantime, they were all to sharpen their French-language speaking skills and start working on articulating **core values** so they'd already have traction when they met for their next meeting.

Course Two—*Potage*

Pronounced "po-taaj," this is the soup course.

. . . .

Vichyssoise—**Potato Leek Soup**
Serves 6-8

Ingredients
    4 cups sliced leeks, white part only
    4 cups diced potatoes, old or baking potatoes recommended
    6 to 7 cups water
    1 ½ to 2 teaspoons salt, or to taste
    ½ cup or more sour cream, heavy cream, or crème fraîche,
        optional
    1 tablespoon fresh chives or parsley, minced

Special Equipment Suggested: a heavy-bottomed,
3-quart saucepan with cover

Note: If you're not puréeing the soup, cut the vegetables
into small pieces.

Preparation

Bring the leeks, potatoes, and water to a boil in the saucepan. Salt lightly, cover partially, and simmer 20-30 minutes or until the vegetables are tender. Purée the soup if you wish. Taste, and correct the seasoning. After chilling the soup, you may wish to stir in a little more cream. Taste again, and carefully adjust the seasoning. Top each serving with a sprinkle of chives or parsley.

Pairing Note

Enjoy this course with Villebois Menetor Salon, a crisp, dry, white wine from Loire Valley, France.

The Banner You Fly

"My mission in life is not merely to survive, but to thrive; and to do so with some passion, some compassion, some humor, and some style."

—**MAYA ANGELOU,** author and poet

For a moment, think of yourself as a business. In our personal lives, a mission statement is the counterpart of a mission statement in the business arena—it's the same.

Have you crafted a clear, concise, and articulate mission statement? It is, after all, the banner you fly! Before crafting your statement, write the top four priorities in your life. Somewhat like a compass, this exercise will help you get your bearings.

My top four priorities are:

- ○ To live a life of simplicity
- ○ To forgive
- ○ To let go
- ○ To make a contribution that's positive, uplifting, constructive, and healing—daily, if possible

Business or personal, a mission statement—banner—should be constructed with materials that withstand all weather, fair or foul: materials such as integrity, honesty, ethics, reliability, and dedication. Intended or not, our mission statement flies every day—expressed—in the way we live.

In my office, I have a carved wood sign that translated from Gaelic means "the work will bear witness;" the work speaks for itself.

When the "widget" we sell or the service we offer speaks for itself, it's a game changer. We don't have to hype it, promote it, or yell about it. Everyone else does that for us. And that's the best type of advertising we can have—word of mouth. It's priceless.

In my profession, I've had ample opportunity to consult with people who desire to make a genuine contribution to society through their company's service or product. As stated at the onset, the purpose of this book is to close the gap between career and spirituality. It's at this intersection that we shine; it's in these crosshairs that we can implement common business practices and strategies to effectively manage our personal growth and success: to live on purpose—*to transform our lives.*

Mission statements aren't just for companies, organizations, or individuals; they can be a guiding compass for blogs as well. A perfect example, "And So It Goes" is the warm and welcoming internet space of returned Peace Corps volunteer Janet Givens, a sociologist and author of the award-winning book *At Home on the Kazakh Steppe.* Simple and to the point, her blog's mission statement is, "To foster curiosity in cross-cultural experiences, both at home and abroad–especially the ones that make us gasp (and laugh)."[23]

My personal mission is to *affect heart-based change.*

Now it's your turn. What's yours?

Leave Your Comfort Zone

Now that we've crafted a mission statement, we want it to be successful. One of the best ways I've found to create productive, long-lasting change is to periodically step outside of my comfort zone. Many times, success begins when we leave our comfort zone.

To do that, you must:

○ *Be clear about your intent and define what you want to work toward.* What do you aspire to?

○ *Do your research.* Before relocating from the Midwest to the Pacific Northwest, my husband and I did two years of research. We looked at several criteria: year-round climate, the cost of living, the quality of life, employment and unemployment rates, and the crime rate. We looked at income tax, property tax, cultural offerings, and even though our child is an adult, we looked at the quality of schools because that speaks volumes.

○ *Face your fears.* Often our fears stem from worry about what others might think about our choices as well as fear of the unknown. Look back at a time in your life when you made a change. Did you feel as though you failed or were successful? Did the change benefit you regardless of the outcome? Did you feel judged or liberated? What's the worst that can happen as a result of leaving your comfort zone? What's the best that can happen?

○ *Stop worrying about perfection ...* fuhgedaboudit! No one is perfect. Understanding that is a huge relief. Why, then, do we spend so much time and energy pretending our lives are perfect? It's exhausting, and when we put that type of pressure on ourselves, we typically come up short.

○ *Accept what happens.* We rarely know what life's going to throw our way. It's unpredictable. The only thing we can control is how we react to what happens to us and move forward. There are times—lots of them—when life is messy. The good news is that while sometimes things go wrong, sometimes they go right.

○ *Expand your circle.* When we associate with the same people day in and day out, we get comfortable. And while comfortable is nice, we don't get a fresh perspective from others to learn from. When we meet new people, we have another frame of reference.

○ *Ask for help.* We become more courageous when we don't have to go at things alone. When we get support and encouragement from our family and friends, it's a winning situation. Find someone you trust, relay your desire and intent to them, and ask for their support. Remember, you've defined your intent, researched the pros and cons of your desire, and are willing to face your fear of change. We don't always have to be brave by ourselves. Despite what society tells us, asking for help and support is one of the bravest, most admirable things we can do for ourselves.

○ *Laugh at yourself.* It's okay to be silly. There's no rule that says once we reach a certain age we can no longer dance in the rain or sing in our car. So the next time it rains, pull a Gene Kelly or Debbie Reynolds; the next time your favorite song comes on in the car, turn it up, belt it out, and own it.

○ *Let your guard down.* If we wear a suit of armor all the time to protect ourselves and to hide our fears and feelings, we'll never allow ourselves to be hurt. If we're never hurt, there's no need to change, right? Hiding behind our armor is the same as hiding behind ourselves. This may work temporarily but leaves us feeling unsatisfied. Sometimes we have to feel discomfort to move forward.

○ *Get out of the rut.* Humans feel an element of control with habits and routines. It's the predictability that keeps us in our comfort zone. We leave our houses at the same time each day. We drive the same route, eat at the same restaurants, and associate with the same people. That's the premise of the movie "Groundhog Day."

What would happen if you changed the smallest thing in your routine? If you took a different route, you might discover a new path. If you left your home a few minutes earlier or later, you might meet someone new in the elevator. If you invite a new colleague to lunch at a new restaurant in town, you might discover you like it, and that your new companion shares the same fears and desires.

The slightest change in your routine might just shift your perspective enough to view things a little bit differently, to see opportunities you missed before, and to open yourself to new possibilities.

"Action expresses priorities."

—**MAHATMA GANDHI,** political and spiritual leader

SECTION THREE

Core Values

La Mandarine Bleue

Course Three—*Poisson*

The Heart of the Matter

Core Values

"If a brand genuinely wants to make a social contribution, it should start with who they are, not what they do. For only when a brand has defined itself and its core values can it identify causes or social responsibility initiatives that are in alignment with its authentic brand story."

—**SIMON MAINWARING,** branding consultant, advertising creative director, social media specialist, and blogger

Core values reflect what an organization or company values; they're a reflection of philosophy, principles, and beliefs. The internal compass of a company, core values help businesses make ethical decisions; they anchor every aspect of a business in a set of commonly held beliefs and commitments and help them keep an eye on the products and services they contribute to the world.

And while a company's overall business plan is monitored, evaluated, and revised, core values don't change; they're lasting—indelible. The following is a list of ten core values that are common across organizations in different industries:

❍ *Accountability*—acknowledging and assuming responsibility for actions, products, decisions, and policies by individual employees and the company as a whole

○ *Balance*—taking a proactive stand to create and maintain a healthy work–life balance for employees

○ *Commitment*—committing to a great product, service, and initiatives that impact lives within and outside the organization

○ *Community*—contributing to society and demonstrating **corporate social responsibility**

○ *Diversity*—respecting variance and offering the best composition of employee background and skill set to get the job done well

○ *Empowerment*—encouraging employees to take the initiative and give their best, even when it means trial and error

○ *Innovation*—pursuing new creative ideas that have the potential to change the world

○ *Integrity*—acting with honesty and honor, never compromising the truth

○ *Ownership*—taking care of the company and customers as if they are one's own

○ *Safety*—ensuring the health and safety of employees and going beyond the legal requirements to provide an accident-free workplace[1]

Let's drill down and look at a few examples of core values from high-profile companies many of us are familiar with.

Trader Joe's

○ *Integrity.* In the way we operate stores and the way we deal with people. Act as if the customer was looking over your shoulder all the time.

○ *Product driven.* Our strategy emphasizes price, product, access, service, and experience. We want to excel at one, be very good at another, and meet customer expectations on the others.

○ *Create a WOW customer experience.* We celebrate the special way we treat and relate to our customers. We think retailing is all about customer experience, and that is what really differentiates us.

○ *No bureaucracy.* We give everyone a license to kill bureaucracy. All offices are in cubicles. The CEO is in a conference room. We have very few layers—a very simple organization.

○ *Kaizen.* [Chinese and Japanese for "continuous improvement"]. Each one of us every day is trying to do a little better. This is infused into our training programs. We really stress teamwork and working together, while we do not elaborate budgeting at the store level.

○ *Treat the store as the brand.* Individual products are not the brand. The store is. Brand is really the covenant between the company and the customer, and the real key is day-to-day consistency in meeting and satisfying needs.

○ *We are a "national/neighborhood" company.* Our customers benefit from our national buying ability, but we want each store to be close to the customer and really a part of their neighborhood.[2]

"There is nothing slick about our stores, on purpose. They are meant to be a unique social experience."

—**DAN BANE,** chairman and CEO of Trader Joe's

Coca-Cola

- ○ *People.* Be a great place to work where people are inspired to be the best they can be.

- ○ *Portfolio.* Bring to the world a portfolio of quality beverage brands that anticipate and satisfy people's desires and needs.

- ○ *Partners.* Nurture a winning network of customers and suppliers, together we create mutual, enduring value.

- ○ *Planet.* Be a responsible citizen that makes a difference by helping build and support sustainable communities.

- ○ *Profit.* Maximize long-term return to share owners while being mindful of our overall responsibilities.

- ○ *Productivity.* Be a highly effective, lean, and fast-moving organization.[3]

"Consumers no longer want only a great product, they want to buy products from companies that align with their own character and values."

—**MUHTAR KENT,** CEO of Coca-Cola

Hewlett-Packard

○ *Passion for customers.* We put our customers first in everything we do.

○ *Trust and respect for individuals.* We work together to create a culture of inclusion built on trust, respect, and dignity for all.

○ *Achievement and contribution.* We strive for excellence in all we do; each person's contribution is critical to our success.

○ *Results through teamwork.* We effectively collaborate, always looking for more efficient ways to serve our customers.

○ *Speed and agility.* We are resourceful and adaptable, and we achieve results faster than our competitors.

○ *Meaningful innovation.* We are the technology company that invents the useful and the significant.

○ *Uncompromising integrity.* We are open, honest, and direct in our dealings.[4]

"When people use your brand name as a verb, that is remarkable."

—**MEG WHITMAN,** CEO of Hewlett-Packard

Sounds True

We are committed to honoring all of Sounds True's stakeholders. This includes:

- ○ *Our authors and artists*. We strive to create relationships with our authors and artists that are based on partnership and transparency, and which are characterized by honest and open communication, equitable agreements, and a commitment to act with care and integrity.

- ○ *Our customers*. We value the intelligence of our customers and are committed to providing them with substantive, genuinely transformative learning experiences. Our titles are carefully produced and beautifully packaged and are backed by Sounds True's 100 percent satisfaction guarantee.

- ○ *Our employees*. Through a positive work environment, health benefits for families, flexible schedules (when possible), and an employee training and assistance program, we invest in the well-being of all Sounds True employees.

- ○ *Our vendors*. We are committed to treating our vendors the way that we want to be treated by other companies—with fair terms and paid on time.

- ○ *Our investors*. We are committed to growing the long-term value of the business through careful planning and re-investing our profits into innovation and growth.

- ○ *Our community*. Through a matching donation program (matching employee gifts to non-profits two to one) and Sounds True's prison library project, we are committed to supporting those who are doing good in our community.

○ *Our earth.* We offset 100 percent of the power we use in our offices with wind energy credits, and we are committed to using recyclable materials to the fullest extent possible in all of our catalogs, books, and packaging.[5]

"The workplace as a crucible for human development . . . a business that is really doing its job is a people growing machine."

—**TAMI SIMON,** founder and CEO of Sounds True

In his *Harvard Business Review* article "Make Your Values Mean Something," Patrick M. Lencioni, founder and president of the Table Group, a management consultant specializing in executive team development, wrote, "Take a look at this list of corporate values: Communication. Respect. Integrity. Excellence. They sound pretty good, don't they? Strong, concise, meaningful. Maybe they even resemble your own company's values, the ones you spent so much time writing, debating, and revising. If so, you should be nervous. These are the corporate values of Enron, as stated in the company's 2000 annual report. And as events have shown, they're not meaningful; they're meaningless.

"Enron—although an extreme case—is hardly the only company with a hollow set of values. I've spent the last ten years helping companies develop and refine their corporate values, and what I've seen isn't pretty. Most values statements are bland, toothless, or just plain dishonest. And far from being harmless, as some executives assume, they're often highly destructive. Empty values statements create cynical and dispirited employees, alienate customers, and undermine managerial credibility."[6]

In their book *Built to Last: Successful Habits of Visionary Companies*, authors Jim Collins and Jerry Porras say, "Core values are the deeply ingrained principles that guide all of a company's actions; they serve as its cultural cornerstones. They're inherent and sacrosanct; they can never be compromised, either for convenience or short-term economic gain."

Different from core values, but equally valid, are three other types of values that a company formally or informally develops. Patrick Lencioni defines them as follows:

"**Aspirational values** are those that a company needs to succeed in the future but currently lacks. A company may need to develop a new value to support a new strategy, for example, or to meet the requirements of a changing market or industry.

"**Permission-to-play values** simply reflect the minimum behavioral and social standards required of any employee. They tend not to vary much across companies, particularly those working in the same region or industry, which means that, by definition, they never really help distinguish a company from its competitors.

"**Accidental values** arise spontaneously without being cultivated by leadership and take hold over time. They usually reflect the common interests or personalities of the organization's employees. Accidental values can be good for a company, such as when they create an atmosphere of inclusivity. But they can also be negative forces, foreclosing new opportunities. Managers always need to distinguish core values from merely accidental ones, as confusion here can be disastrous."[7]

Fifty-five percent of all *Fortune 100* companies claim integrity as a core value, forty-nine percent espouse customer satisfaction, and forty percent tout teamwork. And while those are commendable attributes, there's nothing distinguishing about them. Embracing *en masse* values doesn't set them apart from the competition.

A company that breaks the cookie-cutter mold is Intel. Their employees are pushed to embrace the value of risk taking by challenging the status quo and engaging in constructive confrontation. During orientation for example, "new employees are taught the art of verbal jousting without holding on to hard feelings."[8]

Tony Wild, the CEO of MedPointe, wanted his business to have a unique culture, so working with seven top managers, Wild focused on two core values: *a can-do attitude* and *the tireless pursuit of results*. The group chose those values based on an analysis of a few employees who personified qualities that executives most wanted to see adopted through MedPointe's culture. "As for those employees who can't embrace or embody these values," Wild says, "That's okay. They might be a better fit at another company."[9]

The Golden Thread

You've honed your core values. They're a perfect hand-in-glove fit with your organization. Now what? The golden thread—core values—must be woven through your company's entire fabric.

Business management expert, Patrick Lencioni says, "If they're going to really take hold in your organization, your core values need to be integrated into every employee-related process—hiring methods, performance management systems, criteria for promotions and rewards, and even dismissal policies. From the first interview to the last day of work, employees should be constantly reminded that core values form the basis for every decision the company makes."[10]

So how do you get people to share your core ideology? You don't. You can't.

On his *Strategic Discipline Blog*, author Douglas Wick wrote, "Find people who are predisposed to share your core values and purpose; attract and retain those people, and let those who do not share your core values go elsewhere. Indeed, the very process of articulating core ideology may cause some people to leave when they realize that they are not personally compatible with the organization's core."[11]

> "It's impossible to change the social without changing the personal—you have to put your money where your mouth is. And if you're not making those challenges at home, it's unlikely you'll make them in a larger setting."
>
> —**CARRIE MAE WEEMS**, artist, photographer, and videographer

La Mandarine Bleue

"At the end of the day, it's not the talent of the chef that determines how good a dish tastes, it's the talent of the farmers. Chefs are not the rock stars. Farmers are the rock stars."

—**DOMINIQUE CRENN,** chef and restauranteur

Riding their bicycles, Zoe and Bill were the last to arrive at Yousef and Amina's North End bungalow. Understated on the outside, passersby would never imagine the interior's stylish, elegant, and bold look. The interior's welcome is unforgettable with vibrant colors—the dark red of paprika, the rich browns of cinnamon and nutmeg, and a deep shade of pumpkin—and unconventional pieces, each a unique story of Yousef and Amina's history, a reflective combination of complex personalities. Guests find their home fresh, dynamic, and intriguing.

And though their kitchen is small, the food and flavors that emerge are big and delicious. Seated on Moroccan leather poufs and richly hued plump pillows around a centralized, low-set table, the soon-to-be proprietors of *La Mandarine Bleue* were treated to a bevy of Moroccan delights: everything from tuna *briouats* (small, stuffed pastries) and shrimp *briwats* (like egg rolls) to eggplant fritters and crusty bread cubes served with Moroccan honey hummus, paired with a bold Chilean red wine and served in Moya glasses with their distinctive heavyweight glass stems.

Over the *oohing* and *ahhing* of her guests, Amina said, "Before we discuss core values, I'm dying to hear about the location hunt that Sally, Larry, and Bill have been on. Have you found anything promising?"

Bill and Larry nodded at Sally indicating she be the spokesperson. "Well as a matter of fact," she said theatrically, drumming her fingers on the table, a mischievous smile playing on her lips, "we're working with an agent who has a lead on a place that will be available in a couple of months. Their lease is up, and with low profits, they've decided to close shop. We have an appointment to see it in the morning, but from everything we've seen online and on paper, it looks like it just might fit the bill."

The room erupted in rapid-fire questions: "Where is it?" "What kind of business is currently in it; is it a restaurant?" "What street is it on?" "What's next to it?" "Does it have a view?" "What's the parking like?" "Would we buy or lease?" "How much does it cost?"

Bill stood, both hands up, palms out. "It hasn't been a restaurant for a decade. It's currently a retail store that's not doing as well as they'd hoped. It's in the middle of Restaurant Row, so they thought they'd benefit from the area's foot traffic, but don't.

"The agent said that everything is still in the kitchen. Only the dining area was converted to retail space. Apparently, the back area still has an oven, griddle, a massive commercial stove, and an industrial-size refrigerator-freezer. But we don't know the condition of any of it. It's probably in poor condition and completely outdated. We'll find out in the morning. The line of thinking here is that if we have to update and replace anything, it's already plumbed and wired as a commercial kitchen.

"The parking is the same as all of the other restaurants on Restaurant Row: street parking, first come, first served, with most people using the parking garage. The view is the same as the other restaurants too, the hustle and bustle of 6th Street with a small front area for patio seating in the summer months. There's currently a restaurant on either side.

"Once we see the space, if it seems viable for our purpose, we'll make a follow-up appointment for all of us to see it together and make a group decision to move forward, or not. After our appointment, we'll let everyone know our findings."

As the conversation continued, Sally helped Yousef clear the table while Amina made a pot of Moroccan spiced coffee. As the rich aroma filled the air, Amina returned to the living room with a tray of *makrout*—delicious, cake-like cookies with almonds and honey.

They took turns reading what they'd crafted for the restaurant's core values. Many were similar, and after voting and blending verbiage, they arrived at a concise set of core values for *La Mandarine Bleue*, which, as proprietors, they were proud of and pledged to adhere to.

The Core Values of *La Mandarine Bleue*

RESPECT
We respect and value each person who comes through the doors of *La Mandarine Bleue*, be they guests or staff. We consider their experience and well-being our highest priority.

EXCELLENCE IN HOSPITALITY
We bring the highest level of knowledge and enthusiasm to the job every day. We reflect the best traditions of French hospitality, treating our patrons with grace and courtesy as honored guests in our home.

CULTURAL AUTHENTICITY
We offer a genuine and authentic glimpse of France, honoring the country's traditions through food, art, ambiance, and service. We are proud to provide a truly French atmosphere and to serve dishes with authentic ingredients and preparation.

TEAMWORK AND FAMILY
In France, family and community are an essential part of life. We are proud of the diversity of our staff and the depth of experience and perspectives they bring to us. We believe that we work best when we work together; we support each other in our efforts to learn and grow.

SOCIAL AND ECOLOGICAL RESPONSIBILITY
We are dedicated to maintaining sustainable business practices. We look for opportunities to positively impact our social and environmental surroundings through community giving and advocacy.

ECONOMIC SUSTAINABILITY

We aim to generate a sufficient **return on investment** to sustain operations with a minimum amount of risk. We pursue profit as a means to reinvest in a healthy, vibrant workplace and to create opportunities for further growth and development.

Smiles all around, they'd enjoyed another productive evening and decided that the next step would be to craft goals and objectives and for Peter to research the necessary steps to obtain a liquor license. Until they found a location for *La Mandarine Bleue,* everything else was pretty much at a standstill.

As they were leaving, Bill reminded them, "We'll let you know tomorrow about the space. Have your calendars ready so we can schedule a group walkthrough should it prove promising. *N'oubliez pas de pratiquer votre Français. Allons-y*—Remember to practice your French. Let's go."

Course Three—*Poisson*

Pronounced "poh-son," this is the fish or seafood dish.

Sole Meunière—**Lightly Fried Fish**
Serves 2

Ingredients
    ½ cup all-purpose flour
    4 sole fillets (each about 3 to 4 ounces)
    Coarse kosher salt
    Freshly ground black pepper
    2 tablespoons olive oil
    2 tablespoons (¼ stick) unsalted butter

Sauce
    ¼ cup (½ stick) unsalted butter, cut into 4 pieces
    2 tablespoons chopped fresh Italian parsley
    1 tablespoon fresh lemon juice
    Lemon wedges

Preparation

FISH

Place flour in pie dish. Rinse fish. Pat with paper towels. Sprinkle both sides of fish with coarse salt and freshly ground pepper. Dredge fish on both sides with flour. Shake off excess. Place on platter.

Heat oil in large skillet over medium-high heat until oil is hot and shimmers. Add butter and quickly swirl skillet to coat. When foam subsides, add fish and cook until golden on bottom, 2 to 3 minutes. Carefully turn fish over and cook until opaque in center and golden on bottom, 1 to 2 minutes. Divide fish between two warmed plates. Tent with foil. Pour off drippings from skillet; wipe with paper towels.

SAUCE

Place skillet over medium-high heat. Add butter and cook until golden, 1 to 2 minutes. Remove from heat. Stir in parsley and lemon juice (sauce may sputter). Spoon sauce over fish. Serve with lemon wedges.

Pairing Note

Enjoy this course with Sauternes, a sweet white wine from Bordeaux, France.

The Heart of the Matter

"Living coherently doesn't mean everything is in perfect order all the time. It simply means you are living in alignment with your values and have not sacrificed your integrity along the way."

—**BILL BURNETT** and **DAVE EVANS** from *Designing Your Life: How to Build a Well-Lived, Joyful Life*

For a moment, think of yourself as a business. In our personal lives, virtues—personal character traits that need cultivating—are the counterpart of core values in the business arena.

The seeds are inherent at birth, but it's our job to till, mulch, weed, and water—develop, nurture, and enrich—this part of our inner landscape so they don't lie dormant.

Like anything else worthwhile, tending a garden in our heartspace requires effort and relaxed, creative attention. It's something we do on purpose. *Intentionally.* Being able to define our core values—the crop of virtues we're cultivating—is important because the character traits we embrace help keep our inner ecology vibrant and healthy.

Our personal reputations are a reflection of our core values. In large part, the type of friends we have is determined by them. Core values move us to help family, friends, and strangers—people we don't even know. We continually make behavioral choices that affect ourselves and others. Many of those choices involve matters of right and wrong, and it's difficult to choose to do the right thing without possessing core values.

Below are my personal core values. If you're struggling to craft your own, perhaps reading my list will help you gain traction as you get started.

> **Active Gratitude**—The words gratitude and grace share the same origin, the Latin word *gratus,* meaning pleasing or thankful. In their article "Is Gratitude Good For You? The Evidence on Giving Thanks," The Bronfenbrenner Center for Translational Research defines gratitude as "orientation towards noticing and appreciating the positive in the world."[12] I believe that definition describes *passive* gratitude. If, however, that spark ignites a fire that inspires personal change, that passivity transforms into *active* gratitude. Gratitude in action—intentional—has a broad range of benefits:
>
> ○ **Inward**—Through appreciation we find contentment.
> ○ **Outward**—It inspires generosity—be it our time, skills, or money—and gifts us with opportunities to serve.
> ○ **Environmentally minded**—It's a catalyst for healing our planet through the respect of nature.
>
> Feeling grateful for things we might ordinarily take for granted—our body, the air we breathe, our home, the sky—is a good indication that our spiritual health is in order. For thousands of years gratitude has crossed religious and cultural boundaries as both a social and theological virtue, but it's a relatively new subject in the field of scientific research.
>
> Robert Emmons a psychology professor at UC Davis says, "Grateful people take better care of themselves and engage in more protective health behaviors like regular exercise, a healthy diet, [and] regular physical examinations." His research also revealed that grateful people tend to be more optimistic, a characteristic that boosts the immune system—a clear physical benefit.[13]

Dr. Alex Wood a postgraduate researcher in the Department of Psychology at University of Warwick says, "... gratitude is an integral part of well-being"—a clear benefit to our mental and emotional faculties.[14]

A major component of health and wellness, gratitude helps us to appreciate the blessings we already have, and sparks the anticipatory pleasure of blessings to come. It contributes to opening our heart—the seat of compassion—and helps us to see the benefit in our experience. It enhances trust and helps us to forgive—an unarguable benefit to our spiritual aspect.

"Acknowledging the good that you already have in your life is the foundation for all abundance."

ECKHART TOLLE, author, public speaker, and spiritual teacher

Intentional Kindness—It's not just about being kind; it's about being kind *on purpose*. Two of the best examples of this are doing random acts of kindness and paying it forward.

Random acts of kindness can be small. Here are some real-life examples from my clients. When Paula travels, she makes it a practice to stand up every suitcase that comes down the conveyor belt so they're easier for others to grab.

When Theresa brings her trash cans in from the curb, she brings her neighbors' bins in as well.

When Rita returns her grocery shopping cart to the corral, she makes a point of returning someone else's too.

When Sandra and her husband take their evening walk, they carry bags and pick up litter.

Paying it forward is a concept that involves doing something good for someone else in response to a good deed done for you. When you pay it forward, you don't repay the person who did something nice for you. Instead, you do something nice for someone else. For example, if someone shovels snow from your driveway, you might help someone else change their flat tire.

Our personal **ripple effect** is the power of one generating hope and change in others for a better world. Like ripples radiating across the surface of a pond when a pebble is tossed in, kindness is powerful and has far-reaching, positive ramifications that bring about a tremendous sense of joy.

"Here are the values that I stand for: honesty, equality, kindness, compassion, treating people the way you want to be treated, and helping those in need. To me, those are traditional values."

—ELLEN DEGENERES, comedian, television host, actress, writer, and producer

Active Listening. Without exception, every person is part of a relationship. We're someone's child, and we might be a sibling, parent, partner, coworker, or friend. A vital role in any healthy relationship is listening, so it's no wonder that we have two ears and only one mouth. The design is proportional to the amount of listening and talking we're supposed to do.

Hearing and listening are vastly different. One of the benchmarks of a great communicator is a person's ability to listen not just to what's said, but equally important, to what's not said. An excellent communicator listens between the lines and attends to the other person's unspoken emotions and concerns.

Hearing is passive. We hear dogs bark, tires squeal, trash cans being rolled out to the curb, birds chirp, the mournful wail of a train whistle, church bells ring, and the deep-throated rumble of the furnace when it comes to life in the morning. During a conversation, someone who's hearing instead of listening is often busy formulating their response.

Listening is active. It's something we do intentionally—*on purpose.* It's something we invest ourselves in. When we invest in something, we typically expect a return. When we invest in active listening, the dividend is an expanded capacity for compassion. As a bonus, it can also win friends, improve our relationships, boost our business profits, or advance our career.

Intentional listening includes three fundamental ingredients: respect, validation, and not interrupting others while they're speaking. Respect the other person's perspective—even if we don't share it. Validate their feelings—even if we don't understand them. And let them completely finish what they're saying before jumping in with a response—even if it's a "solution." Remember, not everyone is looking for an answer; often people just want to be heard.

"People start to heal the moment they feel heard."

—**CHERYL RICHARDSON**, *New York Times*
bestselling author

Positive Choices. To celebrate my fiftieth birthday, I went on a brief hermitage. During that sojourn, I asked myself questions such as, Where have I been? Where am I now? Where am I going? And by the way, What is the single most important thing I've learned to date?

During my half a century of living, I'd learned a great many things. But the one truth that kept surfacing over and over again was—and still is—the most important precept that I've learned to date: *Whatever you are not changing, you are choosing.*

What baggage are *you* carrying through life that weighs you down and makes the journey cumbersome and tiring? Is it those extra pounds? Are you in a job you can barely tolerate? Do you fail to keep your promises? Are you staying in a relationship that's bankrupting your heart? Are your spending habits out of control?

I received an email from a woman who found my website and read my observation—*Whatever you are not changing, you are choosing.* She wrote, "The tagline at the top of your site stopped me in my tracks. I can't stop thinking about it. It hit me like a punch in the gut! So hard, in fact, that I copied it and put it on a kitchen cabinet for me to see, read, and remember. Oh, the multitude of situations, choices, and thoughts I could filter through that phrase. And how the choices I make could look different in light of it—in the light of it—because I think it does call us to live in the light of our best intentions. Just eight little words, after all. . ."

The items we choose *not* to change are the same items we tuck into invisible baggage that we carry. People tolerate in life what they subject themselves to.

"I believe the choice to be excellent begins with aligning your thoughts and words with the intention to require more from yourself."

—**OPRAH WINFREY**, media proprietor, talk show host, actress, producer, and philanthropist

Simplicity. A dyed-in-the-wool minimalist, I'm drawn to simplicity, efficiency, and order. *A place for everything and everything in its place.* For me, and others with a similar mindset, outer order contributes to inner calm. We thrive in spaciousness, enjoying the tangible benefits of fewer material items. For us, clearing clutter—be it physical, mental, emotional, or spiritual—brings about ease and inspires a sense of peace, calm, and tranquility.

My creative muse is *wabi-sabi,* a practice where inessentials are trimmed away or eliminated. The intersection where *wabi* (minimal) and *sabi* (functional) meet is the platform for my creativity: space and quiet solitude, simplicity.

During a discussion with my husband he asked, "Just exactly why is it that you need to have empty space around you?" I answered, "Because it appeals to my *zensibilities.*" I meant to say sensibilities, but in retrospect, the word I used fits much better. It's more than being content. For me, it's the enjoyment of less with an awareness and deep appreciation for how less is truly more.

For those who are drawn to simplicity but aren't sure how to start, it's as easy as going through each room of your home and creating three piles: keep, donate, and throw. Once you've removed the donate and throw piles, wait a week and go through the exercise one more time. You may be surprised at what you eliminate on the second go-round. You may feel so light, free, and unburdened that you do it a third time!

Focus on life's simple pleasures that don't require dusting: having your feet rubbed, soaking in a hot bath, having your hair brushed by another person, sleeping in freshly laundered sheets, being lulled by the sound of ocean waves, and enjoying the delicious taste of your favorite food.

Other simple pleasures include long walks or bicycle rides, people watching, cultivating kindness, all ripe with the characteristics of a wabi-sabi lifestyle: simple, yet full; functional; authentic; and imperfect.

"Simplicity, clarity, singleness: these are the attributes that give our lives power and vividness and joy as they are also the marks of great art."

—**RICHARD HOLLOWAY**, writer, broadcaster, and cleric

Let Go. When we release something, not only are we letting go of our hold on it; by default, its hold on us is cut off as well. Depending on the situation, the act of letting go can be extremely healthy. For example, creativity experts tell us that letting go—abandoning control to one degree or another—results in the fun-factor rising in direct proportion to the degree of letting go.

Many of us hold onto things—relationships, places, habits, and emotions—that no longer serve us well.

Sometimes it's out of fear that we allow these attachments to stand in our way, shut down our creativity, and block our joy, yet release is something we repeatedly do throughout our lives.

In parenting, it happens when our child gets on a school bus that first time, again when they move away from home, yet again if they get married—all tearful, emotional events. Repetition doesn't make it easy. Letting go is hard. *Extremely hard.*

Release is multi-layered. It includes grief and grieving, letting go of mistakes, finding and embracing new love, forgiving and receiving forgiveness. The ability to forgive and let go of the past is one of the most critical challenges many of us face.

Forgiveness can be defined as the decision—a conscious choice—to let go of resentment, anger, and thoughts of revenge as a result of real or perceived offense, hurt, or wrongdoing. The reason many people hang on to these is the misplaced belief that to forgive means to condone.

Letting go isn't easy. It involves allowing things to change. It requires an ongoing examination and revision of closely held thoughts and ideas, a continuing willingness to let go.

Now it's your turn. What are your core values?

"Even though you may want to move forward in your life, you may have one foot on the brakes. In order to be free, you must learn how to let go. Release the hurt. Release the fear. Refuse to entertain your old pain. The energy it takes to hang onto the past is holding you back from a new life. What is it you would let go of today?"

—**MARY MANIN MORRISSEY,** life coach, motivational speaker, founder of Life Mastery Institute, and author

SECTION FOUR

Goals and Objectives

La Mandarine Bleue

Course Four—*Entrée*

On Your Mark, Get Set, Goal!

Goals and Objectives

"What you get by achieving your goals is not as important as what you become by achieving your goals."

—**ZIG ZIGLAR,** salesman, motivational speaker, and author

When I had my brick and mortar facility and a new client was coming for their first appointment, I'd send an email confirmation along with directions and a photograph of the building. My small establishment—a Sears catalog kit, circa 1920—was located in the historic district of town. I'd caption the photo, "It's much easier to hit the target when you know what you're looking for."

It's the same with goals. They're much easier to reach when you know exactly what they are. Well-defined goals and objectives keep a successful business on the right track and pointed in the success' direction.

Let's look at the difference:

○ *Goals* are the destination; they define where you're going and when you're going to arrive. They increase effectiveness and are comprised of words (as opposed to numbers).
○ *Objectives* are the map; they're the specific steps you must take to reach your destination. They support goals, enhance efficiency, and often involve numbers and dates.

Goals and objectives are designed to support a company's mission and vision statements.

Sometimes there's a disconnect between establishing goals and achieving them. Why does this chasm exist, and why does it seem to be so prevalent? Maybe it's because our goals and resolutions aren't **SMART**.

The concept of SMART goals is attributed to Peter Drucker, one of the prominent business innovators from the 1960s and seventies.

SMART goals are used in many workplace environments to measure performance during the annual review process. The word SMART is an acronym for the five characteristics of well-designed goals: Specific, Measurable, Attainable, Realistic, and Time-bound.

Using a landscaping business, let's take a look:

○ *Specific.* Goals must be clear, stating expectations such as who, what, when, where, why, and how.

   Example: Increase revenue by fifteen percent each month by landscaping two more yards each month.

○ *Measurable.* If our goals aren't measurable, we won't know whether or not we're making progress toward successful completion. Measurable goals have a numeric or descriptive measurement or milestone to indicate progress.

   Example: Gain two clients each quarter for my landscaping business by participating in a monthly networking group.

○ *Attainable.* Goals must be things that are within reach. If they're set too high or too low, they're meaningless. Since the inception of SMART goals, many companies have modified "attainable" to "aspirational," encouraging their employees to stretch for goals that are slightly out of reach.

   Example: Offer tree trimming services to my clients by October 31. Note: The goal is specific, measurable, and is SMART if there are employees available and with the skills to provide the service.

○ *Realistic.* Make sure the goal is relevant and consistent with the mission; that it represents an objective toward which we're willing and able to work.

Example: Write and submit seasonal articles to local publications regarding foliage issues residents may be experiencing and provide easy-to-implement solutions.

○ *Time-bound.* Goals must have starting points, ending points, and fixed durations. Goals without completion deadlines tend to get consumed by day-to-day interruptions that invariably come up.

Example: Create a business website for my landscaping business by December 31st. Utilize a website development company to create the site and payment interface.

In the corporate environment, a single goal might look something like this:

1. Goal (what)
○ Reduce office supply costs by fifteen percent by the end of the fourth quarter.

2. Tactical Steps (how)
○ Perform audit of supply costs for last twenty-four months.
○ Perform audit of supply usage for last twenty-four months.
○ Identify people or department(s) with the highest supply usage.
○ Identify wasteful usage.
○ Evaluate supplier agreements.
○ Shop suppliers.
○ Negotiate new supply rates.
○ Create standard supply lists and usage guidelines.

The person responsible (who) for each step within a goal, the due date (when), and the status (completed, in process, or not started) are included in a good business goal.

Not only can goals be SMART, Coca-Cola believes in working smart; to:

○ Act with urgency.
○ Remain responsive to change.
○ Have the courage to change course when needed.
○ Remain constructively discontent.
○ Work efficiently.[1]

Success Is Personal

Edith Cooper, Global Head of Human Capital Management at Goldman Sachs is often asked about how she "made it." And while she's happy to share her story, she's quick to point out that she doesn't believe her version of success will necessarily correspond to someone else's. She shares five pieces of advice.

"*Success is personal.* Don't waste energy benchmarking yourself against other people. Rather than try to replicate another person's achievements, determine what is important to you and take it from there.

"*Feedback is not.* If you surround yourself only with people who compliment your strengths rather than call out your weaknesses, you are bound to limit yourself. More often than not, it's your toughest critics who push you toward success. So, when you find someone who tells you the truth about yourself—keep them close.

"*Surround yourself with difference.* It's natural to gravitate toward people who have similar styles, interests, and experiences. While this approach can feel safe, over time, it will stifle growth, limit learning, and impede innovation. Your best ideas are likely to be born from conversations and interactions that occur outside your comfort zone.

"*Pick your spots.* You're not going to be great at everything every single day. Be clear about your priorities—to yourself and those close to you—and know that some days you'll be the hero at work, and some days you'll be the hero at home. And that's OK.

"*People remember people.* I've been fortunate to work alongside highly motivated and highly talented people throughout my career. Many of these folks have been among the best in their respective fields. As I look back now, what I remember most about individuals is not the revenue they produced or the titles they held—it's the interactions that we had and whether our relationship was based on trust, respect, and collaboration."

She goes on to say, "While these lessons have served me well, what I try to emphasize to others is—it's not about how I made it to 'the top'—it's about what you will do when you get there."[2]

"At Goldman Sachs, our firm is itself in a period of transition, with new leaders emerging and longstanding ones saying goodbye. Our workforce is nearly seventy percent millennial—even our latest partner class is composed of eleven percent millennials, and of course, that number will only increase as the years go by."

—**EDITH W. COOPER,** Executive Vice President and Global
    Head of Human Capital Management at Goldman Sachs

La Mandarine Bleue

"My philosophy from day one is that I can sleep better at night if I can improve an individual's knowledge about food and wine, and do it on a daily basis."

—**EMERIL LAGASSE,** celebrity chef, restauranteur, and cookbook author

Even with the agent's reminder that the location hadn't been a restaurant for more than ten years, Bill and Sally couldn't help but feel incredible disappointment at the sight of the property on 6th Street. Larry was aghast. The space meant to serve as the dining area was garish. They agreed that no amount of paint or special lighting could diminish its vulgarity. And it wasn't just the physical structure. It felt wrong; the vibe was eerie.

The kitchen was horrible. The room itself was sizable, but the oven was a relic, like something unearthed in an archeological dig. The massive range was filthy and caked in congealed grease topped with layers of dust and liberally sprinkled with mouse droppings. None of them were willing to open the ancient refrigerator in the event it was hiding a body.

Larry kept his hands tight to his chest afraid that if he touched anything he'd get a disease. They unanimously agreed that unless the entire place was gutted and rebuilt, this wasn't the place. And it went without saying that a rebuild would cost a fortune.

Bill made it crystal clear to the agent—whose face betrayed the embarrassment he felt—that in the future, a personal walk-through on his part before scheduling an appointment with them was imperative for an ongoing relationship. They'd had such high hopes and weren't looking forward to sharing this setback at the next meeting.

Because they live only two blocks away, Larry and Dwayne walked and were the first to arrive at Sally's charming, old-world style home. Everyone else opted for bicycles and showed up *en masse* shortly after that.

Though small, Sally's home has a big feel with high ceilings and beautiful birch floors. On their way to the back deck where she does most of her entertaining, they passed through her bright, immaculate kitchen with its granite counters, shaker-style alder cabinets, and stainless appliances. The kitchen reflects her luminous yet no-nonsense personality. Sally cheerfully instructed, "Grab a plate and glass on your way through."

Her extensive deck boasts warm, caramel-colored rattan furniture with gently angled backs, welcoming wide arms, and jewel-toned throw pillows in emerald, sapphire, and ruby. To ensure no one got chilled, Sally had lit the Venetian-style, wood-burning chiminea. The smell added to the rich, Tuscan atmosphere. Amina, a self-proclaimed fire bug, claimed a seat nearby so she could feed it wood as necessary.

Bill got right to the point. "The property on 6th Street sounded too good to be true. And it was."

Peter asked, "You mean difficult to believe?"

As she came through the sliding door holding a food-laden tray, Sally affirmed, "It was unbelievable all right. Unbelievably awful!"

All eyes followed the massive tray, which she placed on the low-set center table. The tray was loaded with a variety of finger foods including baked zucchini cups with gorgonzola cheese, mini pearl tomatoes, and fresh basil and Tuscan tomato-basil-garlic bruschetta with diced artichokes, Kalamata olives, and capers. It also had antipasto kabobs with Italian meats, cheeses, olives, and pickled vegetables skewered in bite-sized pieces and grape gorgonzola truffles rolled in toasted nuts.

A successful marketing executive, it was no secret that Sally often availed herself of the services of one of her clients, the most popular catering company in the greater Boise area. During a rare moment of silence—when everyone's mouths were busy enjoying the delicious food—Sally said, "I'll be right back. I'm going to get the wine." She returned with two bottles of robust, inky dark Malbec from Cahors in Southwest France. After a liberal pour into each glass, she said, "I'd like to propose a toast. Here's to a hearty *no*, which puts us that much closer to our yes. *A bientôt!*"

Setting down his glass, Peter said, "In researching the liquor license, I've learned it'll be slow going until we have our physical space because much of it depends on our location. Once we've got that, it's full steam ahead."

Unlike the previous meeting when they'd crafted their core values, this time when they went around the table to share potential goals, the enthusiasm was lackluster. Dwayne said what they were all feeling, "It feels canned; mechanical."

Yousef said, "In preparing for our meeting I read an article that said 'Google doesn't set annual goals beyond those required by the SEC.' Apparently, they feel it decreases their agility, the ability to respond to what the market's doing."

"In the research I did to try to write goals, I read that single-minded FOCUS—Follow One Course Until Successful—on a goal can make a person oblivious to reality and unable to deal with changes to their market or environment," Dwayne added.

Sheila, who'd been absorbed by the conversation, asked, "Does defining goals define our limitations?"

Peter turned to her in stunned appreciation, "Wow, I'd never thought about it like that."

Shifting her gaze away from the mesmerizing flames of the chiminea, Zoe chimed in, "What I'm hearing is that we don't want to be tied to a shoulda-woulda-coulda list of bullet points driven by externals. We want our goals to be a natural result of something that's internal and aligned with who we are.

"Our values are a perfect reflection of that: respect, excellence in hospitality, cultural authenticity, teamwork and family, social and ecological responsibility, and economic sustainability.

"What if our goals were simply to live our core values and be our personal best every day?"

Smiling, the group voted unanimously they would follow Zoe's suggestion.

"On that note," she said, "let's meet at our house next time. Our homework is to continue looking for a location. Bill, Sally, and Larry, will you still spearhead that?"

"Absolutely," the trio agreed.

"Peter will resume liquor license research once we've got our space. And since we know we want to be somewhere in the Old Boise Historic District or Central Downtown area, I—and anyone who wants to join me—will scope out the competition." Grinning she added, "It's a tough job, but somebody's got to do it."

Making their way back through Sally's house, the guests saw the dimly lit living room, which revealed an airy, natural design highlighting Sally's love of simple, clean lines with furnishings and artwork that radiate her warm personality and energy: positive, energetic, and cerebral.

Waving them off the front porch, Sally reminded everyone, "We all need to continue to *la pratique de notre Français*—practice our French."

Course Four—*Entrée*

Pronounced "aun-trey," this term can be confusing. In the United States it typically means the main course. In other parts of the world, however, it's the course that's served immediately prior to the main course.

. . . .

Pavés du Mail—Pan-Fried Steaks with Mustard Cream Sauce
Serves 4

Ingredients
- 4 (8–10-oz.) flat iron steaks, cut horizontally without the connective tissue
- Kosher salt and freshly ground black pepper, to taste
- 1 tablespoon unsalted butter
- 1 tablespoon canola oil
- 5 tablespoons cognac or brandy
- ¼ cup heavy cream
- 1 ½ tablespoons Dijon mustard
- 1 tablespoon minced flat-leaf parsley

Preparation

Season steaks with salt and pepper. Heat butter and oil in a 12-inch, cast-iron skillet over medium-high heat. Add steaks and cook, turning once, until browned and cooked to desired temperature, about 6 minutes for medium-rare. Remove pan from heat. Transfer steaks to four warm plates and pour off and discard all but 1 tablespoon fat.

Add 4½ tablespoons cognac to pan and stir, scraping browned bits from the bottom with a wooden spoon. Return pan to medium-high heat and cook for 20 seconds. Add cream and mustard; season with salt and pepper; and cook, stirring vigorously, until sauce just comes together. Stir in remaining cognac and pour sauce over steaks. Serve steaks garnished with parsley and black pepper.

Pairing Note

Enjoy this course with Mourvèdre, a red wine grown in many regions around the world including the Rhône and Provence regions of France.

On Your Mark, Get Set, Goal!

"One of the lessons that I grew up with was to always stay true to yourself and never let what somebody says distract you from your goals. And so when I hear about negative and false attacks, I really don't invest any energy in them, because I know who I am."

—**MICHELLE OBAMA,** first African-American First Lady, lawyer, and author

For a moment, think of yourself as a business. In our personal lives, goal-setting is the counterpart of goals and objectives in the business arena—it's the same.

Many times, not always, personal goals come in the form of resolutions. Plaza College in New York posted the top ten New Year's resolutions for 2012:

- ○ Spend more time with family and friends.
- ○ Fit in fitness.
- ○ Focus on weight loss.
- ○ Quit smoking.
- ○ Enjoy life more.
- ○ Quit drinking.
- ○ Quit smoking.

○ Learn something new.
○ Help others.
○ Get organized.[3]

And while these goals are worthy, "An estimated forty percent of Americans make New Year's resolutions (more than the total number of people who watch the Super Bowl). Yet, according to research from Dr. John Norcross at the University of Scranton, only eight percent actually achieve them.

"There is also a steep drop-off in terms of length of commitment to these resolutions. Seventy-five percent of resolutions are maintained after the first week. Yet, by the second week of February, as much as eighty percent of resolution makers are dealing with the 'remorse of disappointment' (though, if you are in your twenties, you are almost four times more likely to stick with your resolutions than if you are over age fifty)."[4]

Though I don't make New Year's resolutions—I pick a single, positive focus word instead—I do set personal goals. After a presentation I gave at a women's retreat I received an email asking me what my personal goals are. I replied with the following list of desires to which I aspire.

You'll notice that they're *daily* aspirations. When measured against the SMART goal criteria, they're specific, measurable (either I am or I'm not), attainable, realistic, and time-bound to each day of my life. Some lifelong desires can be achieved daily.

If you haven't formulated personal goals yet—desires, aspirations—perhaps you could use some of the following as seed thoughts to help you get started:

○ Keep the energy in the package I reside—my physical body—healthy and balanced.
○ Accept and respect myself and others "as is."
○ Be authentic; always.
○ Be a positive, uplifting, constructive, and healing influence.
○ Be present; show up for life with reverence and a sense of wonder.

- ○ Live my purpose: a mindful agent of heart-based change.
- ○ Listen "between the lines," and be sensitive to what people aren't saying.
- ○ Integrate the wisdom I have with the life I live.

But what if your goals miss the mark?

Failure IS an Option

> "My attitude has always been, if you fall flat on your face, at least you're moving forward. All you have to do is get back up and try again."
>
> —**RICHARD BRANSON,** business magnate, investor, and philanthropist

Stanford University's most popular class, Designing Your Life, is taught by Bill Burnett and Dave Evans. In it, they say, "One of the principles of design thinking is that you want to 'fail fast and fail forward,' into your next step." It's not to avoid failure. In fact, failure can be a launchpad for creativity." They go on to say, "Failure is just the raw material of success."

In his book *How to Fail at Almost Everything and Still Win Big: Kind of the Story of My Life* Scott Adams the creator of the Dilbert comic strip wrote, "This is a story of one person's unlikely success within the context of scores of embarrassing failures. Was my eventual success primarily a result of talent, luck, hard work, or an accidental just-right balance of each? All I know for sure is that I pursued a conscious strategy of managing my opportunities in a way that would make it easier for luck to find me."

When I received an invitation to be part of a group of beta testers who would discover whether or not people could "click their way to happiness," I accepted with enthusiasm. As a holistic health practitioner and transformational life coach, this type of research is of tremendous interest to me because many of my clients are recovering from major setbacks—closed doors.

Positive psychology and positive neuroscience based on the study founded by neuroscientist Dr. Richard Davidson at the Center for Investigating Healthy Minds at UW-Madison was delivered online to each beta tester in the form of interactive games, activities, and exercises designed to help the user sift through their experiences and find opportunities for gratitude, growth, and to optimize their well-being.

The science of happiness shows that failure is an option. *What matters is how we respond to it.*

Researchers concluded that we enjoy a higher quality of life when we experience a certain number of setbacks—five to seven of them. Why? Because setbacks give us confidence that we can weather adversity, and they reinforce what we truly value. For example, health and loving relationships, which can result in enhanced priorities and different goals.

On the other hand:

○ Too many setbacks can break our spirits.
○ Too few setbacks can protect us from developing resilience.

Resilient people tend to "make meaning" as they face and overcome challenges. This allows them to discover positive outcomes that wouldn't have presented themselves if the problem hadn't occurred. This is called BeneFinding—finding benefit in negative experiences.[5]

In their book, *Shift Into Thrive: Six Strategies for Women to Unlock the Power of Resiliency*, authors Lynn Schmidt and Kevin Nourse wrote, "The ability to thrive in the midst of adversity [resiliency] is not a given; it is an intentional choice. Make the choice today to thrive."

What was the last benefit you found from a negative experience?

In an interview with the Santa Clara Valley Historical Association, this was Apple founder, Steve Jobs', response to failure:

"I've always found something to be very true which is that most people don't get experiences because they never ask. I've never found anybody that didn't want to help me if I asked them for help.

"I called up Bill Hewlett when I was twelve-years-old. He lived in Palo Alto, and his number was still in the phone book. He answered the phone himself saying 'Yes?'

"I said, 'Hi, I'm Steve Jobs, I'm twelve years old, a student, and I want to build a frequency counter. I was wondering if you have any spare parts that I could have.'

"He laughed, and he gave me the spare parts to build the frequency counters, and he gave me a job that summer at Hewlett-Packard on the assembly line that built frequency counters. I was in heaven.

"I've never found anyone who said no or hung up the phone when I call and just ask. And when people ask me I try to be responsive and to pay that debt of gratitude back.

"Most people never pick up the phone and call; most people never ask. And that's what separates, sometimes, the people who do things from the people that just dream.

"You've got to act. And you've got to be willing to fail; be willing to crash and burn with people on the phone, with starting a company, with whatever.

"If you're afraid of failing, you won't get very far."[6]

"Keep yourself motivated. You've got to be motivated, you've got to wake up every day and understand what that day is about; you've got to have personal goals—short-term goals, intermediate goals, and long-term goals. Be flexible in getting to those goals, but if you do not have goals, you will not achieve them."

—**GARY COHN,** investment banker, President and COO of Goldman Sachs

SECTION FIVE

Market Segmentation and Targeting

La Mandarine Bleue

Course Five—*Relève*

You Are the Company You Keep

Market Segmentation and Targeting

"What helps people, helps business."

—LEO BURNETT, advertising executive, named by *Time Magazine* as one of the 100 most influential people of the twentieth century

A marketing offer consists of a combination of information, experience, services, or products that satisfy a need or want in the marketplace.

Leo Burnett was responsible for some of the most recognized ad campaigns in the United States including Tony the Tiger, Charlie the Tuna, the Marlboro Man, the Maytag Repairman, United's "Fly the Friendly Skies," and Allstate's "Good Hands." He also garnered multinational clients such as McDonald's, Hallmark, and Coca-Cola. Burnett knew that the purpose of *marketing* in the business world is to promote a product or a service. The purpose of *public relations* is to promote goodwill toward the company and its product or service.

Equally important to the business plan is a marketing plan—a written description of the current market position of a business and its marketing strategy for the period covered by the plan, usually one to five years.

But before any of that happens, a company does its **due diligence** by segmenting and targeting. From a large marketplace, they extract smaller populations of consumers with similar requirements, needs, and interests.

Market segments can span a population from birth, into toddler-hood, through the "tweens," into teens, and into adulthood and include various targets therein: ethnicity, gender identity, sexual orientation, academic and income levels, spiritual traditions, relationship status, the list goes on.

Once research is complete, companies develop marketing and pro-motional strategies that target a particular group's tastes and financial capacity.

For example:

○ *Tara Motors* launched Tata Nano for consumers in a lower income group (segment).
○ *Ray-Ban* caters to a high-income group.
○ *Nokia* understands their target audiences well and offers handsets for different segments: men, women, and teenagers.[1]

If a company seeks outside funding for their enterprise, the bank and investors require a comprehensive marketing plan that consists of several elements:

○ Market Positioning and Strategy
○ Marketing and Selling Model
○ Product Launch
○ Operations and Organization
○ Financial Analysis

"Hope is not a marketing plan."

—**MICHAEL BOEZI**, strategist, educator, and author

A marketing plan also includes market segmentation and target-ing. Marketers use a variety of methods to reach their ideal—often called "target"—market. Each method must be relevant, appealing, and memorable to the ideal audience. Ads need to be distinctive, pointing to the benefits that make the product desirable to consumers, and explain how the service or product is better than competing brands'.

From the early days of radio and television advertising, there has been on-going debate about the ethics of targeting advertisement to minorities (youth markets, especially young children) and protected segments such as racial minorities, women, and seniors.

Highly controversial is the role ethics plays in market segmentation and targeting, yet marketers contend that customer segmentation is vital because it saves times and resources and provides the best investment return of the marketing budget. But does that make it right?

Marketers apply tremendous effort to reach specific sectors of society. Attempts to reach these groups may result in the use of stereotypical perceptions in their campaigns. For example, an ad for a product in one geographic area reflects the racial group where it's promoted while the same ad used in a different location is done with actors who resemble that population.

Companies that do this run the risk of offending a group and inadvertently exposing themselves to lawsuits or even more financially devastating, the **court of public opinion**.

In their article "Target Marketing and Ethics Brand Advertising and Marketing Campaigns," authors Gyongyi Fogel and Lorinda Less say, "Marketing to a targeted minority can provide a competitive advantage for an organization. However, there are ethical and legal concerns that must be carefully evaluated.

"Youth, children, and protected minorities, including women and the elderly, are a high target of advertising because of the increasing importance of these segments in making purchasing decisions. Recent population and demographic factors continue to impact marketing to address minority marketing issues with careful attention to ethics and social responsibility."[2]

Marketers have a long track record of identifying, understanding, and targeting particular consumer segments with advertising geared to entice them to purchase specific products, yet the public remains concerned with the ethics—or lack thereof—of targeting potentially vulnerable consumers with products that may cause economic, physical, or psychological harm.

When investigating consumer vulnerability, frequently considered attributes include age, gender, ethnicity, education, and socioeconomic status.

"When they go low, we go high."

—**MICHELLE OBAMA**, first African-American First Lady,
lawyer, and author

History offers a plethora of incidents when companies crossed the line from customer segmentation into the realm of discriminatory marketing. Case in point, R.J. Reynolds Company and their attempt to launch a new brand of cigarette called *Uptown*.

A *New York Times* article titled "A Cigarette Campaign Under Fire" says, "Here in the root and stalk of tobacco country [Winston-Salem, North Carolina], everyone knows that marketing something that carries a health warning from the Surgeon General is bound to provoke an argument. Mix in race, and you really have a shouting match. Just ask the R.J. Reynolds Tobacco Company."[3]

More recently, corporate scandals involving ethics include firms such as Enron, Tyco, and WorldCom. Let's take a brief look at each.

Enron—In a *Forbes* article titled "Enron, Ethics and Today's Corporate Values," author Ken Silverstein wrote, "Enron's heyday has long ended. But its lessons will long endure. The global business community is now watching a painful new chapter in this saga—one where its former high-riding chief executive officer, Jeff Skilling, is getting a decade shaved off of his prison term that should now end in 2017.

"The company's failure in 2001 represents the biggest business bankruptcy ever while also spotlighting corporate America's moral failings. It's a stark reminder of the implications of being seduced by charismatic leaders, or more specifically, those who sought excess at the expense of their communities and their employees. In the end, those misplaced morals killed the company while it injured all of those who had gone along for the ride.

"'Just as character matters in people, it matters in organizations,' says Justin Schultz, a corporate psychologist in Denver.

"Surely, if there are profits to be made, some type of scheme that attempts to skirt the law or even cross boundaries will occur. It's been that way throughout history. But with each passing scandal, new rules and codes emerge that surpass those of the past. And while Enron won't be the last case of corporate malfeasance, its tumultuous tale did initiate a new age in business ethics.

"Enron, once a sleepy natural gas pipeline company, grew to become the nation's seventh largest publicly-held corporation. But its shoddy business practices, aided by bankers and advisors feeding from the gravy train, brought down the company in December 2001."[4]

Tyco—NBC News reported, "Dennis Kozlowski, the former CEO of Tyco International Ltd., and former Tyco finance chief Mark Swartz were sentenced Monday to up to 25 years in prison for stealing hundreds of millions of dollars from the company.

"The sentences end a case that exposed the executives' extravagant lifestyle after they pilfered some $600 million from the company including a $2 million toga birthday party for Kozlowski's wife on a Mediterranean island and an $18 million Manhattan apartment with a $6,000 shower curtain.

"Kozlowski, 58, and Swartz, 44, were convicted in June after a four-month trial on 22 counts of grand larceny, falsifying business records, securities fraud, and conspiracy.

"Kozlowski and Swartz are the latest executives sentenced to prison in a wave of white-collar scandals that shook corporate America and outraged the public after thousands of people lost their jobs and pension nest-eggs."[5]

WorldCom—CBS News reported, "The stock markets got another king-sized jolt as WorldCom revealed what could turn out to be one of the biggest accounting scandals in U.S. history.

"The telecommunications company said it had fired Chief Financial Officer Scott Sullivan, and accepted the resignation of senior vice president and controller David Myers, after an internal audit found improper accounting of more than $3.8 billion in expenses over five quarters.

"The misstated billions are also very bad news for ordinary WorldCom workers: 17,000 of them will be fired, with layoffs beginning on Friday.

"The company's shares, among the most heavily traded on Wall Street in the past few months, fell as much as seventy-six percent in after-hours action following the announcement and at one point were trading at twenty cents each. In January, they were trading at about $15.

"'This is why the market keeps going down every day—investors don't know who to trust,' said Brett Trueman, an accounting professor at the University of California, Berkeley's Haas School of Business, in an interview with CBS MarketWatch. 'As these things come out, it just continues to build up.'"[6]

Corporate scandals have negatively impacted the public's perception of who they can and can't trust. Discriminatory marketing, stealing, lying, grand larceny, fraud, and conspiracy have brought about the implosion of many high-profile companies and brought the question of ethics to the forefront of consumers' minds. But there remain people with integrity. Case in point, Andrew and Mark Madoff.

Remember the Bernie Madoff scandal in 2008 when he tricked investors out of $64.8 billion through the largest Ponzi scheme ever? Madoff told his sons, Andrew and Mark, about his scheme; they reported him to the SEC and he was arrested the next day. Madoff got a 150-year prison sentence and had to pay $170 billion in restitution.

Before Andrew's death from cancer, he blamed his relapse on stress and humiliation from the scandal. Mark committed suicide on the second anniversary of his father's arrest.

In an email to the *New York Post*, Madoff wrote, "As difficult as it is for me to live with the pain I have inflicted on so many, there is nothing to compare with the degree of pain I endure with the loss of my son's [*sic*] Mark and Andy. I live with the knowledge that they never forgave me for betraying their love and trust."[7]

> "Corporate executives and business owners need to realize that there can be no compromise when it comes to ethics, and there are no easy shortcuts to success. Ethics need to be carefully sown into the fabric of their companies."
>
> —**VIVEK WADHWA,** technology entrepreneur, academic, fellow at the Rock Center for Corporate Governance, and author

Compassionate Consumerism

Many consumers specifically look to buy from companies that are socially responsible. They want their products and services to come from businesses that demonstrate high ethical standards in everything they do: from sourcing to product packaging and everything in between.

An ever-growing number of companies desire to apply practices in their daily work that support a sustainable operation in harmony with the natural environment through the principle of Reduce—Reuse—Recycle. They strive to reduce their environmental footprint in their local, state, and global communities while maximizing their profit potential.

In his TED talk, psychologist Daniel Goleman said, "The objects that we buy and use have hidden consequences. We're all unwitting victims of a collective blind spot. We don't notice—and don't notice that we don't notice—the toxic molecules emitted by a carpet or by the fabric on the seats. Or we don't know if that fabric is a technological or manufacturing nutrient; if it can be reused or does it just end up in a landfill?

"In other words, we're oblivious to the ecological and public health and social and economic justice consequences of the things we buy and use. In a sense, the room itself is the elephant in the room, but we don't see it. And we've become victims of a system that points us elsewhere.

"There's a wonderful book called *Stuff: The Hidden Life of Everyday Objects*. And it talks about the back story of something like a t-shirt; it talks about where the cotton was grown and the fertilizers that were used and the consequences for the soil of that fertilizer.

"It mentions, for instance, that cotton is very resistant to textile dye; about sixty percent washes off into wastewater. And it's well known by epidemiologists that kids who live near textile works tend to have high rates of leukemia.

"There's a company, Bennett and Company, that supplies Polo.com, Victoria's Secret—they, because of their CEO, who's aware of this, in China formed a joint venture with their dye works to make sure that the wastewater would be properly taken care of before it returned to the groundwater. Right now, we don't have the option to choose the virtuous t-shirt over the non-virtuous one. So what would it take to do that?

"There's a new electronic tagging technology that allows any store to know the entire history of any item on the shelves in that store. You can track it back to the factory. Once you can track it back to the factory, you can look at the manufacturing processes that were used to make it, and if it's virtuous, you can label it that way. In other words, at point of purchase, we might be able to make a compassionate choice."[8]

Companies tailor their marketing messages to enhance persuasion. When planning an ethical marketing strategy, it's important to research which segments may be interested to know that your company complies with ethical standards. For example, a cosmetics company that markets "earth-friendly" products might state that they don't test on animals.

Forbes says that "Corporate social responsibility (CSR) means demonstrating a concern for human rights, the environment, community development, and employee rights."[9] An example of CSR is Starbucks; they're known for being a socially responsible company due to their commitment to coffee farmers who adhere to environmental best practices.

Businesses can enjoy a higher rate of brand loyalty from consumers who care about ethical factors if the business informs their market.

Fast Company—a business magazine that focuses on technology, business, and design—says, "Consumers may discriminate against a brand because of ethical concerns. Win their loyalty by being the company that adheres to high ethical standards. Promote the fact that you do it, and enjoy a competitive advantage because of it."[10]

Leveraging Vulnerability

Have you ever noticed that while marketing campaigns deliver ads to consumers in a positive, upbeat style, the underlying premise targets a sense of lack—vulnerabilities?

- My house isn't big enough.
- My car isn't fast enough.
- My teeth aren't white enough.
- My hair isn't bouncy enough.
- My body isn't slender enough.
- My skin isn't smooth enough.
- My neighbor has a boat, but I don't.
- My co-worker vacations in exotic locations, but I don't.

"You can be the moon and still be jealous of the stars."

—**GARY ALLAN**, country music artist

La Mandarine Bleue

> "When seasonality is reimagined as a grocery list rather than a limitation, everyday meals become cause for celebration—a whole week of fresh sweet corn; a blue moon autumn asparagus harvest; a rich, spicy soup made with the last few sweet potatoes of winter."
>
> —**ANDREA REUSING,** chef and leader in the sustainable agriculture movement

Sally was the first to arrive at Bill and Zoe's Harrison Boulevard home. Already outside talking with their gardener, Zoe left Bill to his animated conversation to welcome their first guest. A beautiful day, the two women visited on the columned front porch while waiting for the others to arrive.

Yousef, Amina, Peter, and Sheila arrived on bicycles followed by Larry and Dwayne in their British-racing-green Mini Cooper, complete with two white bonnet stripes.

Passing the gently curved spiral staircase, they entered what Zoe refers to as "the great room," a vast space the muted hue of Grey Poupon mustard and trimmed in crisp, edelweiss white. The hardwood oak floors gleamed in the natural light that streamed through the French doors flanking the glassed-in marble fireplace.

Three cream-colored sofas casually arranged in a loose semi-circle sat atop a vibrant, Turkish rug that Bill and Zoe had acquired while on one of their many adventures. Perfectly paired accent pillows mirrored the spirited colors making the room cheerful and welcoming.

"Shall we get right down to business or eat first?" Bill asked.

"Eat!" came the unanimous answer.

"I thought as much," Bill said smiling. "You know the drill. Our kitchen is self-serve, so help yourselves at—" there was a mass exodus before he could complete the sentence. "—will," he finished the sentence to the empty room.

The massive kitchen hummed with appreciative *oohs* and *aahs*. A chef's dream, the enormous space is home to workspace galore; a huge, farm-style oak table; and bar seating. The recessed lighting and eggshell cupboards and walls add to the light and airy feel.

They started with two salads. One contained Greek cheese, mint, pistachios, and honey-lime glaze drizzled over spinach leaves, and the other was an Italian pasta salad with artichokes, garbanzos, parmesan, and basil.

Keeping it light, also on offer were grilled squash, sweet peppers, and asparagus topped with balsamic syrup, sea salt, and red chili flakes, all paired with a delicious red Corbières from the Languedoc-Roussillon region in France. The group ate in quiet appreciation then got ready to discuss business.

"Bring your glasses and let's move to the living room. I'll serve the cake," Zoe said nodding toward her signature dessert—a chocolate lava cake with salted caramel—"when the business portion is done." Knowing they were in for a treat, the friends grinned at each other and headed for the living room.

"First, let's raise our glasses to the space we found for *La Mandarine Bleue* and to our brilliant attorney who guided us smoothly through lease contract waters that could otherwise have been choppy."

"*A bientôt*—cheers!" they rang out in unison.

Bill continued, "The location is perfect. Now for the remodel. At least we're moving forward now. As agreed, I've applied for the business license."

Sally added, "After scoping out the competition, we know that the global array of food choices on 8th Street is what draws clientele—a benefit, not a deficit. The area offers Italian; German; American. . ." She paused and drew a dramatic breath before continuing. "Mexican; Latin; Brazilian; Basque; Greek; and East, South, and Southeast Asian cuisine *plus* a multitude of fusions. The addition of *La Mandarine Bleue* will be the *pièce de résistance*! And since our ideal customers are people over twenty-one with a penchant for excellent wine, we won't have to look far to find them."

Peter jumped in. "Speaking of wine, I love that we've agreed to use the area around the spiral staircase to store and display our selection. That's going to be visually stunning as well as practical. And by the way, now that we've got our location, I'm working with the city clerk. Our liquor license is in the works. I also want to point out that if we ever decide to cater, it looks like there's a separate license required for that.

"I'm currently comparing prices of high-end stemware at restaurant supply stores, but I haven't ruled out working with Libbey Glassware on a direct, wholesale basis. I like how durable and stable they are. They just feel great in the hand. I'll bring samples, and we'll put it to a vote once I've gathered the numbers."

Amina chimed in, "Yousef and I are working on two color palettes. Once we present them to the group and vote, we'll begin looking at tableware and artwork. We're already creating a playlist of soft, French-inspired music."

"Tomorrow morning I'm taking final measurements to confirm our seating count in the dining area so we can start looking at tables and chairs," Yousef added.

Zoe turned to Sally. "Before we leave, let's be sure to check our calendars and schedule a date to talk about advertising and marketing."

Turning to Larry, Bill asked, "By the next meeting can you give us a total on the appliances we'll need for the kitchen?"

"Absolutely. And while we're talking kitchen, why don't we have the next meeting at our house," he said looking at Dwayne for confirmation. "That way we can serve some menu ideas we've been testing using recipes we picked up during our last trip to Provence."

"I'll bring what I've found so far regarding *maître d'* station podiums," Sheila said. "They're available in two sizes: thirty-six and forty-two inch." Turning to Yousef she asked, "Once you've finalized measurements in the dining area, will you please let me know which size will be the best fit?"

"Consider it done," he said smiling.

Standing, Zoe said, "*Suivez-moi à la cuisine pour le dessert.*" Excepting Larry, everyone looked at her with blank stares. "Clearly you haven't been practicing your French. I just said, 'Follow me to the kitchen for dessert.'" She grinned as they stampeded past her and were greeted by the scent of brewing coffee, a perfect accompaniment to her to-die-for cake.

"Good thing we rode our bikes," Amina said smiling through a mouthful of heaven on a fork. "I need the exercise to burn off these decadent calories. Zoe, this is simply delicious!" Everyone agreed.

"We've all got our marching orders for next time," Peter said. "Bill, before I forget. Here's the receipt for the liquor license. And so none of us ever miss out on dessert, let's continue to *pratiquez notre français*— practice our French."

Course Five—*Relève*

Pronounced "ri-lafe," this is the main course, the *pièce de résistance*.

....

Chicken Française—**Lemon Garlic Chicken**

Serves 4

Ingredients

4 boneless, skinless chicken breast halves, pounded thin

1 cup all-purpose flour

1 teaspoon salt

½ teaspoon black pepper

3 large eggs, beaten

¼ cup olive oil

½ cup dry white wine

½ cup chicken stock

3 tablespoons fresh lemon juice

¼ cup butter

Salt and pepper, to finish

¼ cup chopped, fresh parsley

Cook's Note

This recipe calls for dry white wine. Use a good quality wine that you enjoy drinking. The rule of thumb for cooking with wine is never to use something you wouldn't drink.

Preparation

Heat the olive oil in a large skillet set over medium-high heat.

Stir together the flour, salt, and pepper. Dredge the chicken breasts in the flour mixture making sure to coat the whole surface of the chicken. Shake off any excess flour; there only needs to be a thin coating of it on the chicken. Quickly dip the chicken in the eggs and allow any excess egg to run off.

Place the prepared chicken in the heated oil and fry the chicken breasts for 2 to 3 minutes on each side until the meat is cooked through and golden brown. Remove the chicken pieces and place them on a triple layer of clean paper towels to drain. Loosely tent the chicken with foil to retain the heat.

Pour off and discard the remaining oil in the skillet. Deglaze the pan over medium-high with the white wine, chicken stock, and lemon juice, scraping up any browned bits left over from the chicken. Place the butter, parsley, and salt and pepper to taste, in the pan and reduce the heat to medium. Allow the sauce to simmer and thicken until it can coat the back of a spoon. Strain the sauce through a fine sieve and pour into a clean frying pan.

Place the fried chicken into the lemon sauce and allow it to warm through for a minute, turning once. Transfer the chicken to a serving plate. Drizzle any remaining sauce over the chicken breasts and serve immediately.

Pairing Note

Enjoy this course with Sancerre, a white wine produced in the area of Sancerre in the eastern part of the Loire Valley, France.

You Are the Company You Keep

"Surround yourself with the dreamers and the doers, the believers and thinkers, but most of all, surround yourself with those who see greatness within you, even when you don't see it yourself."

—**EDMUND LEE,** social media strategist, entrepreneur, speaker, and author

For a moment, think of yourself as a business. In our personal lives, **personal branding** is the counterpart of market segmentation and targeting in the business arena.

I remember the first time I heard the saying "guilty by association." It came in the form of a warning from my parents. I don't know if it prevented me from continuing with my plans, but the spirit of the adage has remained with me.

The people we surround ourselves with reflect our values, and impressions of us are developed based on our actions and inactions. Good, bad, or indifferent, we're judged by what we say, what we do, what we fail to do, and the people we associate with.

In their book *Millennial Reboot: Our Generation's Playbook for Professional Growth* authors Kate Athmer and Rob Johnson share some of the best, most succinct advice I've ever read that can be applied to our business and personal lives: "Don't be a dick." They followed that with, "Recognize when it's you who's being the asshole," which is the perfect segue to personal branding.

The term "personal branding" is thought to have been first used and discussed in a 1997 article by Tom Peters.[11] Cultivating a personal brand (how you appear to the world) is just as important today as it was then. Even more so because in today's high-tech world, we leave a **digital footprint** viewed by family, friends, neighbors, colleagues, and—depending on security settings—people we don't even know.

Personal branding isn't about tooting our own horn. It's about being the best version of ourselves. It's about being a person who adds value and is authentic, mindful, and relevant—a person who's intentional about their "trademark," a poster child for the values they embrace.

1. How do you conduct your life?
2. What are your parameters?
3. What are your ethics and practices?
4. What will you become involved in?
5. What will you refrain from becoming involved in?

According to a survey conducted by the Glenn Llopis Group, "Less than fifteen percent of leaders have defined their personal brands and less than five percent are consistently personifying them."[12] Why? Perhaps because it can be extremely challenging and requires a tremendous amount of self-awareness, action, and accountability.

The Practice of Excellence

Many people's personal brand includes the practice of excellence. When I was a young girl, I desperately wanted to play the piano. I can remember begging my parents for piano lessons, and then came the wonderful day when they acquiesced and said yes.

The piano phase of my young life was short-lived because I didn't realize that playing the piano involved practicing the piano. I mistakenly expected instant gratification, but it didn't happen in the blink of an eye, and there were no shortcuts in sight.

There're a multitude of things we can practice: various sports, musical instruments, writing, yoga, law, singing, meditation, art, selfless service, medicine, and relationships to name but a few.

The people I find myself drawn to are the people who practice excellence, who embrace practice as the place of transformation. In this mindset, they regard life as their practice and practice as their life. They view everything they encounter through the lens of love.

To become exceptionally good at something we have to practice every single day. To be a master, we have to make it a way of life. Practice is the way we move forward. Once we get there, it's the way we stay.

In yoga, *abhyasa* is having an attitude of persistent effort to attain and maintain a state of stable tranquility. Slow, steady change—breath by breath, asana to asana, still point to still point—until it becomes fluid, efficient, and second nature.

As an adult, I show up for practice—life—in a meaningful way. I choose to live on purpose. The funny thing is, it doesn't feel like practice. It feels like uncovering, discovering, and learning.

Over the years I've learned that practice—life—can be messy. It's here we learn from our mistakes. I've also learned that practice—life—can be cooperative and noisy. It's here we learn from each other. Purposeful practice keeps it all moving forward toward greater clarity and mastery.

In the personal branding wheelhouse, we also find:

○ *Accountability*—taking responsibility for our decisions and actions; having the integrity not to shift blame elsewhere.

○ *Commitment*—the capacity to focus, stay on task, and keep our word. Some people confuse commitment with being involved. The business fable of the chicken and the pig is one of the best illustrations of that confusion. Picture frying eggs and sizzling bacon side-by-side in the hot, stove-top skillet. It's clear to see that the chicken is involved, but the pig is committed.

❍ *Say no* to people, places, things, and experiences that aren't in line with your personal or business direction.

❍ *Invest time, don't spend it.* How we use our time is how we're either spending or investing our life.

Before engaging in activities such as watching reruns on television, staying in a job you can't stand, or remaining in a relationship that's bankrupting your heart, you can ask yourself, "Is this worth exchanging my life for?"

Life! That's a pretty steep price to pay. That's why I opt for activities that are investments—something that yields a return, a dividend. It might be health from exercise, laughter from sharing time with friends, fulfillment from writing, relaxation from a nap, or peace of mind from meditation.

One of my clients, Paul, eventually came to the conclusion that he can allow himself experiences for the mere joy of them. Before that, he felt guilty for doing things "for the joy of it." He said his mindset was such that he didn't deserve them and they would, therefore, be self-indulgent.

I shared with him that doing something for the mere joy of it—for ourselves or others—is quite possibly one of the best returns on an investment of time that a person can receive.

"Some would argue that you're as successful as the company you keep. Certainly, there is a connection between our friends and who we are."

—SIMON SINEK, marketing consultant, motivational speaker, and author

SECTION SIX

Competitive Environment

La Mandarine Bleue

Course Six—*Sorbet*

Keeping Up with the Joneses

Competitive Environment

"Whether it's Google or Apple or free software, we've got some fantastic competitors and it keeps us on our toes."

—**BILL GATES,** business magnate, co-founder of Microsoft, entrepreneur, investor, philanthropist, and author

Competitive analysis is the process of evaluating the competition in the environment where your company operates or where you hope to establish your business.

A healthy practice done by small and large companies alike, this type of analysis includes a comparative review of strengths, weaknesses, and marketplace customers. An excellent analysis also includes identifying strategies that can enhance your position, obstacles that hinder you from entering new markets, and boundaries you can establish that limits others from diminishing your position in the competitive arena.

To think that a business doesn't have competition is naïve. Every business has competition. Every business needs competition. It's the competition that provides benchmarks against which companies can measure themselves. Studying competitors helps companies determine their opportunities for revenue and profitability.

There are several components in a competitive analysis. For each item listed below, a company must decide if their business is at an advantage or disadvantage.

1. Define the competition. Who are they? Do they pose a current or future threat to your company's financial well-being?
2. Identify the competition's advantages and strengths.
3. Determine the competition's vulnerabilities and weaknesses.
4. How does your sales force stack up to the competition's?
5. How does your inventory stack up against the competition's?
6. Do you have what customers want and need? Their priority must become your priority.
7. Is the market already saturated with your product or service?

After sifting through the results and determining if it's in your company's best interest to move forward, you then move to strategic planning that includes production, distribution, pricing, and marketing—all covered in other chapters.

We would do well to listen to two cautionary voices about resting on the laurels of competitive analysis:

In his book *Fatal Illusions: Shredding a Dozen Unrealities That Can Keep Your Organization From Success* James Lucas says, "As long as we appear to be doing better than someone else, we can feel that we must be doing well, so we don't need to change. These illusions can begin when we compare ourselves with our own past performance, or with the performance of other organizations. The companies we're comparing ourselves to may all be performing at lower levels than the market requires. They may all be doing it wrong. Since every organization is unique, another company's solutions may not apply to us.

"Effective strategy formulation and implementation relies on concepts like uniqueness, differentiation, and standing out in a very, very crowded marketplace. Ineffective strategy formulation and implementation relies on concepts like imitation, caution, and blending in with the rest of the pack. Competitive analysis does a great job in fostering the latter. I have no problems in performing a quick, occasional scan of what today's competitors are doing. That is just plain prudent management. The problem is that executives can easily wind up sinking big resources and becoming hypnotized into tracking the movements of today's solutions for yesterday's customers."

In his article "The Hypnotic Danger of Competitive Analysis," business professor Oren Harari wrote, "Traditional competitor analysis is often shortsighted in depth, range, and possibility. If you're spending a lot of valuable time tracking your competitors' movements, you're not only running in circles, but you're probably paying too much attention to the wrong guys. It's the folks that you can't track—the ones that don't exist yet either as competitors or even as companies—who are your real problems. That's because they're not worried about tracking you. They're moving ahead with new offerings, redefining and reinventing the marketplace as they go along."[1]

> "The competitor to be feared is one who never bothers about you at all, but goes on making his own business better all the time."
>
> —HENRY FORD, founder of Ford Motor Company

From Dead Ends to Endless Possibility

In our business and personal lives, there are times when we do a comparative analysis and feel we don't match up, that we're lagging behind. Perhaps we've made decisions that have placed us at a distinct disadvantage, knocked us behind the eight ball.

It's not uncommon for me to hear a client say, "I feel like I'm painted into a corner." When we find ourselves in that position, nine times out of ten, we've but to look in our own hand to see that we're the one who's holding the paintbrush.

Intended or not, it's our choices that shape the future to our personal specifications. The outcomes not only include body, mind, and spirit; they include relationships, career, and finances.

We all know that life is a series of choices and consequences. It takes a series of choices to get painted into the corner; it takes a series of different choices to get back out.

Prevention is the best medicine for staying out of corners. But if we happen to find ourselves wedged into the proverbial ninety-degree angle, there's a way to get out. Ask yourself this question: What is the *greatest* moment of the *greatest* thing I've *ever* been part of?

When we think about the energy—the drive, passion, effort, elation—behind our greatest moment, and compare it to the energy in the painted corner, there's usually a large gap. Think Grand Canyon.

Physicists tell us that we live in a world filled with possibilities driven by probabilities that are affected by observation and attention.

If you haven't thought about the energy behind your greatest moment and its relationship to the energy you're expending today then you're not using what you observed there—in the greatest moment—to affect your current probability and possibility.

Modern-day yogi, visionary, teacher, author, and businessman Leonard Orr says, "Personal law is simply the thought that controls your mind and your life more than any other thought. Finding that thought is the most valuable knowledge that you can have about yourself. It is like the leverage on personal change. It enables you to change very efficiently."

Fear, anger, and jealousy are fulcrums that can leverage us from Point A to Point B, but when those emotions are sustained too long they become debilitating. When we develop the habit of relating the energy of our greatest moment into the energy of our current moment, we find ourselves leveraging power—power that opens the door to unleashed and unlimited potential and possibility.

"Every morning brings new potential, but if you dwell on the misfortunes of the day before, you tend to overlook tremendous opportunities."

—**HARVEY MACKAY,** businessman, syndicated columnist, and author

La Mandarine Bleue

"To me, the interesting part of cooking is bringing flavors *out* of ingredients, not having to put flavors *in*."

—**DIANA KENNEDY,** Mexican cooking authority
and author

Visiting Larry and Dwayne's home is a coveted experience; add dining to the event, and you are in for a lovely treat!

The exterior of their Hyde Park home hints at a noble, rich history. Inside, the timeless beauty of modern aesthetics speaks volumes—culture, fresh, well read, charismatic, subdued elegance—and clearly demonstrates their attention to comfort and entertaining.

"Make yourselves at home. Larry's on his way with *hors d'oeuvres*, and if you'll excuse me, I've got wine breathing in the kitchen."

Turning to admire the living room Sally said, "I love their color scheme. And," nodding to the welcoming espresso-colored sofas, merlot-red chairs, and sage green ottoman and over-sized coffee table in the center that anchors the space, she continued, "their use of big swaths of solid color."

Zoe admired the cool metal touches that give the spacious room a sophisticated air: the ornate mirror, the legs of the coffee table, and the fireplace andirons are all glossed in silver.

Larry and Dwayne entered, drawing Zoe's attention away from the chic surroundings. Larry placed a large, round tray on the center table. Dwayne distributed a small stack of plates and napkins before returning to the kitchen. A mouth-watering scent filled the room.

"Here we have a variety of mini crepes," Larry said. Pointing to a serving dish he continued, "These are filled with zucchini, spinach, and goat cheese. These," he said redirecting his audience's attention, "are filled with ratatouille." And once again shifting his guests' focus, he said, "These are filled with chicken and creamed mushrooms."

Returning from the kitchen with a tray of elegant stemware and two bottles of wine, Dwayne said, "Under Peter's tutelage, I've paired the crepes with a Sauvignon Blanc from the Loire Valley in France." After pouring a glass for everyone, Peter said, "I propose a toast to the contractors who are making tremendous headway." Raising their glasses, it was unanimous. "A bientôt—cheers!"

While everyone enjoyed the savory crepes, Amina interjected, "I did some research, and I'd like to get your thoughts on having two miniature tangerine trees flank the door at La Mandarine Bleue. Not just because of our restaurant's name but because of their significance. In feng shui, they're considered an activator of good chi and a symbol of good luck and financial prosperity. Later when Yousef and I present the color palettes, you'll find that they harmonize beautifully with either one."

Zoe smiled and said, "I think that's an excellent idea!"

"I do too," echoed Bill.

"Who's going to take care of them?" Sheila asked, a hint of doubt in her tone.

Larry, nodding toward Dwayne, answered, "You've all been raving over the crepes. The herbs are from Dwayne's garden. He's fond of saying that cultivating our little herb garden is therapeutic and helps him to word-smith his books. Tangerine trees might provide even more inspiration."

Dwayne nodded in agreement, "I'd love to learn more about miniature tangerine trees. I'd be willing to give it a go."

Every glass empty and not a crumb left on the tray, Larry suggested they adjourn to the dining room.

Larry and Dwayne's gift for hospitality and love of entertaining is clear with one look at their dining room. A mix of traditional and antique pieces with ten Louis-style chairs surrounding a massive table, the room is light and airy with textured whites, creams, and a single wall bathed in pistachio green and home to a huge beveled mirror that serves to warm and expand the space.

Once everyone was seated, Larry explained, "And though I'm in the process of enticing a French chef from Coeur d'Alene, for today's meeting I'm head chef. Dwayne is sous chef, and we'll both be serving. Tonight's meal is representative of the type of menu we'll offer at *La Mandarine Bleue*. Peter helped us pair the wines."

With the confidence and grace of a professional, he went on. "Let me share this evening's menu with you now:

"We're starting with a traditional French onion soup: a slice of baguette covered with emmental cheese paired with Cave de Pomerols, a crisp white wine from Languedoc, France.

"The pear salad features fresh greens and candied pecans, topped with crumbled blue cheese, dressed sparingly with French vinaigrette. This is paired with Chateau de Segries, a red from Côte du Rhône, France.

"The *cassoulet*, *flageolet* and white beans cooked with ham shanks, sliced duck sausages, and carrots, is paired with Xavier Châteauneuf-du-Pape from Rhône, France.

"This evening's dessert is blueberry *crème brûlée* served with *café au lait*."

In the kitchen, Larry and Dwayne laughed at the sensual moans coming from their guests as they enjoyed the first course.

"At least let us carry our plates into the kitchen," Bill said when they'd finished their meal. "I've got to do something to burn calories or Zoe's going to have to push me home in a wheelbarrow."

"I think I'm going to die," groaned Peter. "But what a way to go," he finished.

Making their way to the living room, they prepared to conclude the evening with their business meeting.

"Yousef, did you decide if I should order a thirty-six or forty-two-inch *maître d'* station podium?" Sheila asked.

"Thirty-six inch would be best," Yousef answered. "Speaking of measurements, we have comfortable room for eight round tables that seat four each and four square tables that seat two each, for a total of forty seats in the main dining area.

"In the side area reserved for overflow, private parties, corporate meetings, small conferences or seminars, we can comfortably seat twelve tables of four, for an additional forty-eight people.

"The fire marshal gave us the go-ahead for a guest capacity of one hundred, so we're in compliance. We could fit in seating for twelve more, but then we'd lose the comfort factor and possibly make serving more challenging. I recommend we cap it at eighty-eight."

Everyone agreed with his recommendation adding the caveat that the number could be revisited at a later date should the need for expansion arise, a problem they'd love to have.

Peter said, "I found an excellent wine importer and distributor that's headquartered in Seattle and has a satellite warehouse in Boise. With no minimum requirements, we can place orders on our terms not theirs. And our liquor license goes into effect opening day. We have the go-ahead to serve alcohol at our private, pre-opening event as long as we don't charge for it. I explained to the clerk that the evening will be complementary for our guests.

"Speaking of alcohol, I brought wineglass samples for your vote." Reaching into a bag by his feet, Peter retrieved and carefully unwrapped a tissue-papered lump. "You can see this beautiful glass has a stem, and while the initial cost is less, once stem breakage is factored in, they end up costing more in the long run."

Exposing another glass, he said, "This is a stemless version. It's sophisticated, stylish, and will showcase our wines beautifully. Because it's stemless, the risk of breakage is minimized, and its ergonomic shape is comfortable to hold. The specially designed rim is chip-resistant to withstand daily use.

"No matter which style we decide on, we still need to order champagne glasses, and I suggest we order some stemmed wineglasses for backup because there will be those few customers who insist on that style. But my recommendation is that we go stemless."

Due to their practicality, the vote for stemless was unanimous.

Bill turned to Larry and asked if he'd had the opportunity to work up a total for the cost of kitchen appliances. Every face blanched at the number he delivered, but they'd known it was going to be large. It came in second to remodeling.

Amina and Yousef stepped out briefly and returned from their car with two covered canvases. Standing in front of the group, Yousef said, "The French, true to their individualistic style, interpret color in their subtle way. Paler colors are milky but have depth. Intense colors are vibrant but don't shout."

Amina unveiled the first canvas explaining, "This palette includes soft yellow, powder gray with a hint of blue, and creamy white." Pointing to another swatch of paint, she continued, "Bold accents of cobalt-blue including glazed ceramic pots to hold the miniature tangerine trees, would be stunning."

Unveiling the second canvas, she said, "This palette includes distressed turquoise, daffodil yellow, and bright white." She continued, "It will also harmonize with accents of cobalt-blue."

Putting it to a vote, they decided on the first palette because it was softer and seemed more likely to encourage lingering conversations over wine, dessert, and *café*.

"Another great meeting," Bill said. "Let's meet at our place next time and continue moving forward with our assigned projects."

As the group prepared to leave, Zoe said, "Sally and I have an advertising and marketing meeting set for tomorrow morning at Alia's Coffee House on Main Street."

Waving goodbye to Sally, she said, "I'll see you there at nine."

Closing the door behind their departing guests, Larry and Dwayne turned and smiled at each other. Another successful evening was behind them. Hand in hand, they bypassed the kitchen in an unspoken agreement that the dishes could wait until morning.

Course Six—*Sorbet*

Pronounced "sor-bay," this is a gentle, resting course.

. . . .

Sorbet Poire Cardamome—**Cardamom Pear Sorbet**
Serves 8

Ingredients
    ½ cup granulated sugar
    1 ½ cups water
    ¼ teaspoon ground cardamom
    4 ripe pears, peeled, cored, and chopped
    1 teaspoon fresh lemon juice
    2 tablespoons *eau de vie de poire*, or pear brandy

Cook's Note
Eau de vie de poire serves two purposes in this recipe. It adds a lovely accent of complex flavor to the sorbet, and the alcohol in it prevents the mixture from hardening into an ice block.

Preparation
In a small saucepan, bring the sugar and water to a boil. Reduce the heat and simmer, uncovered, for about

5 minutes until the mixture reduces in volume and thickens. Chill the syrup for at least 30 minutes until it is slightly cool. Process the syrup, cardamom, pears, lemon juice, and pear brandy in a blender until the mixture is smooth. Strain and then freeze the pear puree in an ice cream maker according to the manufacturer's instructions.

Pairing Note

Enjoy this course with Pineau des Charentes, a white wine produced in Poitou-Charentes, France.

Keeping Up with the Joneses

"Never underestimate the power of jealousy and the power of envy to destroy. Never underestimate that."

—**OLIVER STONE,** screenwriter, film director, and producer

For a moment, think of yourself as a business. In our personal lives, comparing ourselves to others is the counterpart of analyzing the competition in the business arena. It's an unhealthy practice that doesn't benefit anyone and can be detrimental. Theodore Roosevelt said, "Comparison is the thief of joy."

A photograph taken during the 2016 Olympics shows Michael Phelps displaying a laser-focus toward finishing. It captures the essence of determination; it portrays the epitome of a winner.

Next to Michael in the photograph is a competitor glancing at him to gauge where he stands. That comparison cost him his focus. The quote that's become tied to that now-famous photo is, "Winners focus on winning, losers focus on winners."

During childhood, we start comparing ourselves to others. At an early age it can help us make sense of things, to figure out how the world works and how we fit in it. Continued comparison with others as adults stems from our life not lining up with our essence, our core. It's a disconnect between where we are and where we want to be—our highest self.

To reconnect we need to look inward. It's here we discover and embrace a liberating concept—comparing ourselves to others isn't necessary.

It's been said that the only person you should compare yourself to is who you were yesterday. When we're the only person we're competing with, we can set actionable, rewarding goals for ourselves.

A Shift in Perspective

Let's shift our perspective for a moment and look at the flip side of the Joneses coin, the healthy side.

"What other people think of you is none of your business."

—**STEPHEN HOPSON**, inspirational speaker, author, and
the world's first deaf instrument-rated pilot

In *Note to Self: A Seven-Step Path to Gratitude and Growth* I share the following story:

"In the booth behind me at a restaurant, two women were having a conversation. One of them said, 'I tend to think too much about how other people perceive me. However, in recent months I've thought, be yourself. No one can tell you you're doing it wrong.'

I wanted to stand up and cheer. Being yourself is a powerful experience to have. Being who we authentically are—a unique expression of source energy—frees us from being held hostage by the opinion of others. I've discovered that the longer I live, the easier it is to let go of what people think of me.

When we inhabit our own life—stop doing things based on the approval of others—we offload baggage and trade up to joy!"

Also known as baby's tears, there's a plant called *mind-your-own-business*. According to the Horticultural Society, "This plant is a native of Corsica and Sardinia, is seen year round, and readily colonies in crevices in dry stone walls."[2] Solid, all-season advice, we'd do well to take a page from this plant's name and mind our own business.

Ours is the only life we can control; comparisons are an exercise in futility. They deplete energy, are a time suck and a waste of two of the most precious commodities we have.

> "A flower does not think of competing with the flower next to it, it just blooms."
>
> —ZEN SHIN

Soul in Bloom

When purchasing a plant from a nursery, we typically receive a care information card that includes instructions for planting, lighting, watering, and feeding so the plant has the best chance to thrive in its new location. If we deviate from the instructions, the plant can't live up to its full potential.

As human beings, we have several aspects of our lives to care for: physical, mental, emotional, and spiritual. Most of us have the physical dimension down pat—we feed, exercise, and rest our body when it needs it. But what about the mental, emotional, and spiritual aspects?

Somewhat like a building, our body is the structure we reside in. And while it's incredibly important, the interior—inner landscape—is even more so. The ecology of our internal space is vital to the quality of our existence, our human experience.

Joy and peace of mind begin and reside in the heart. Like seedlings, they must be nurtured to grow and flourish. Part of the cultivating process includes weeding—a task that's necessary for a healthy garden.

> "Let us be grateful to the people who make us happy; they are the charming gardeners who make our souls blossom."
>
> —MARCEL PROUST, novelist

Weeds are a gardener's nemesis. They vary depending on geographic location, but the most common garden weeds include crabgrass, pigweed, chickweed, lambsquarters, and purslane. Not limited by geographic location, internal weeds include frustration, impatience, bitterness, anger, and guilt. Deeply rooted, they can take over and choke out the blooms and blossoms of joy, hope, and peace of mind.

A well-tended inner environment enhances our ability to experience unlimited potential and possibility, to explore our understanding of who we are and to fulfill our life's purpose. The return on investment for internal self-care is tremendous. It yields riotous blossoms, vivid with the beautiful colors of gratitude, self-acceptance, love, forgiveness, patience, and kindness.

Poet May Sarton wrote, "Gardening is an instrument of grace." May you know the joy that comes from sharing bouquets from your heart. Happy gardening!

A Sense of Wonder

Do you inhabit life with a sense of *meh*—indifference—or a sense of wonder? Are you open to and curious about how the magic of life unfolds and to seeing the world through the lens of appreciation and amazement? This approach to life gifts me with lessons that positively impact my life moving forward. One such takeaway is that life happens *for* me not *to* me.

You might think this is just another day in your life. It's not just another day; it's the one day that's given to you—today. It's a gift, and the appropriate response is gratitude. If you do nothing but cultivate that response to the gift of this unique day, if you respond as if it's the first day and last day of your life, then you have used this day well.

Engage your senses—touch, taste, hearing, smell, vision—to cultivate a sense of wonder. As I write this, I'm in Montana's Bitterroot Valley. *Big Sky Country!* There's so much to enjoy. When I look out the window I often see magpies, pileated woodpeckers, or mule deer passing by. Located between the Bitterroot Range and Sapphire Mountains, I'm a stone's throw from a fisherman's paradise, the Bitterroot River. The cloud formations are exquisite, the snow-capped mountains are breathtaking, the wind can be fierce, and the people are friendly.

I make a point of looking at the faces of people whose paths I cross, knowing that each one has an incredible story behind it, a story I could never fully fathom—not only their story but the story of their ancestors. Just thinking about that boggles my mind. My response is to look them in the eyes and smile. And almost without fail, I receive one back.

"We shall never know all the good that a simple smile can do."

—**MOTHER TERESA,** Catholic nun and missionary

SECTION SEVEN

Definition of Offering

La Mandarine Bleue

Course Seven—*Rôti*

Lay Your Cards on the Table

Definition of Offering

"My definition of 'innovative' is providing value to the customer."

—**MARY BARRA**, CEO of General Motors Company, and first female CEO of a major global automaker

A business product or service offering is vital to marketing efforts. To be effective, a company must first determine their unique **value proposition** and **niche**—and how it compares to the competition—in the marketplace.

A company's offering affects a customer's decision to purchase from them or a competitor. Some businesses offer many goods or services—a product mix—to their clients. A hair salon, for example, doesn't just cut, color, and style hair. They also sell goods and accessories that support the style once a customer leaves: shampoos, conditioners, curl boosters, curl tamers, frizz busters, spray, and hair gel, blow dryers, combs, brushes, clamps, clips, the list goes on.

Hair salons are an example of businesses with *depth*—the number of products or services available in each product line. They're also a good illustration of *width*—the number of product lines available in their offering.

But the offering isn't enough. It's the people representing the product or service that wins—or loses—customers. Their view of the role they play in the big scheme of things makes an impact—positive or negative—on potential customers.

The Merriam-Webster dictionary defines "occupation" as "the work that a person does; a person's job or profession." Example: "His uncle was a tailor by occupation." Synonyms: calling, employment, game, lay, line, profession, trade, vocation, work.[1]

During my two-year research stint at the everything-under-one-roof superstore, I conducted an informal survey asking one hundred employees from entry-level to management, in every department (people who'd occupied their roles for at least one year) the following question, "Do you love, like, tolerate, or hate your job?" The answers were a good indicator of how engaged or disengaged they were.

In their book *Designing Your Life: How to Build a Well-Lived, Joyful Life* authors Bill Burnett and Dave Evans indicate that the more disengaged you are, the more "work equals a kind of dull misery."

These are the results from my informal survey question, "Do you love, like, tolerate, or hate your job?"

ANSWER	NUMBER OF RESPONSES
Love	5 (highly engaged)
Like	28 (engaged)
Tolerate	58 (disengaged)
Hate	9 (highly disengaged)

When asked, "Do you feel that your employer is taking full advantage of your skill?" Seventy-four percent answered no.

When asked, "Do you find the tasks and responsibilities in your job description engaging?" Sixty-seven percent answered no.

When asked, "Why do you come back each day?" The two most popular responses were "paycheck," and "benefits."

Without prompting, several respondents mentioned that they felt stuck, underrated, and unheard—even when they spoke up. Little was said about company culture.

Whether keeping appointments, running errands, or checking items off my *ta-dah* list, I interact with people every day. Here are some of the occupations of the people whose paths I crossed in 2016:

Ophthalmologist

Musician

Hairstylist

Dog groomer

Homemaker

Gas station attendant

Real estate agent

Event Planner

Bookstore staff

Financial advisor

Department of Motor Vehicles clerk

Custodian

Yoga instructor

Landscaper

Teacher

Car mechanic

Office supply clerk

Shoe repairman

University program director

Beekeeper

Journalist

Buddhist monk

Post office clerk

Retiree

Attorney

Florist

House sitter

Photographer

Caterer

Dental hygienist

Tour guide

Bank teller

Bicycle mechanic

Gardener

Park ranger

Hospice volunteer

Writer

X-ray technician

Restaurant server

Uber driver

Flight attendant

Restauranteur

Artist

Apple bar genius

Veterinarian

Cruise ship bartender

Student

Flight instructor

Dog walker

Vintner

Car wash attendant

Carpenter

When asked "Do you love, like, tolerate, or hate your job?" the responses I received, just like their occupations, were all across the board.

The Genius Bar

One of the most enthusiastic responses I received to that informal survey question was from an Apple employee at the Genius Bar. While I was sitting there, the customers on either side of me were equally engaged with their geniuses. "What's up with that?" I wondered.

A bit of research led me to a Finding Mastery podcast titled "Lee Clow: Creative Genius, Loving, Listening," In this engaging conversation between Michael Gervais and advertising guru, Lee Clow, Clow said, "When I grew up surfing, wearing a Hap Jacobs t-shirt was something that I wanted to be part of who I was.

"That was Hap Jacobs telling his brand story through the young kids that wore his Jacob surf team t-shirts, his boards, the logo that was on the board, the logo that was on the store.

"When we did the stores for Apple, we were sitting around talking about the Apple Store, and I recited this whole thing about Jacob surfboards.

"I wanted to be part of that brand.

"We'd surf all morning in South Bay, and then we'd go up to the Jacobs Surf Shop, and we'd hang out in the store and get to know the shapers, and get to know Hap if he was there, and talk about surfing.

"The Genius Bar that's part of the Apple Store was born out of that conversation about wanting to be so much a part of the brand that you can go talk to the purest perpetrators of that brand.

"Hanging out in Jacobs Surf Shop and talking to the shaper was kind of like going to the Apple store and getting an appointment with the Genius Bar to talk about, 'how I can do photos better or whatever you were interested in.'"[2]

The reason I love Apple products is that Apple loves Apple products! Their dynamic offering took me from prospective customer to loyal brand advocate.

"Never expect that your startup can cover every aspect of the market. The key is knowing what segment will respond to your unique offering. Who your product appeals to is just as important as the product itself."

—JAY SAMIT, digital media innovator, pioneered advancements in music, video distribution, social media, and eCommerce

La Mandarine Bleue

"I love that pasta isn't bound by any particular type of sauce. It can be plain and simple, and it can also be rich and complex. It can take on the identity of any country's flavor profile."

—**NIKI NAKAYAMA,** chef and restauranteur

Stepping into Alia's Coffee House a few minutes before nine, Zoe was warmly greeted by Sally who'd arrived just minutes before. Enticed by the heady fragrance of fresh-baked goods and coffee, they stepped to the counter and placed their orders before sitting at one of the many rustic wooden tables.

Across from each other, they opened their laptops, connected to the complementary Wi-Fi, and got down to business. Sally said, "Working with the color palette we agreed on, I started designing our website. I just sent you the link. Take a look."

Even with placeholders for the logo and photos, Zoe was impressed by what she saw. "I love the inviting old chateaux feel of it; it's warm and casual. And the drop-down tabs at the top are easy to navigate and cover everything."

"We've got some serious traction," Sally agreed, "but it still has a long way to go. The social media links don't work yet." She looked up and smiled at Zoe. "I'm hoping you'll set up a Facebook page and Twitter and Instagram accounts. We also need to establish *La Mandarine Bleue* on Yelp and TripAdvisor. Are you comfortable taking those on too?"

When their names were called, they picked up their orders. Sally and Zoe both appreciated the large, hand-warming mugs and leaf designs artfully swirled by the baristas into the foam on top of their drinks. Both women tore into their flakey, golden croissants releasing fragrant steam from the soft insides.

"I've been working on our logo," Sally said wiping a bit of foam from her top lip. Reaching into her supple leather briefcase, she continued, "Close your eyes for a minute. I'm going to lay four potential designs on the table, and I want you to tell me which one grabs your attention first. Ready?"

Eyes closed, Zoe nodded. She heard Sally move both laptops out of the way and the rustle of paper. "Okay, you can open your eyes now."

Each design was exquisite, but the one that grabbed her attention was a small tangerine tree in a cobalt-blue pot. The leaves were bright green, and all of the tangerines were a vivid, reddish-orange with the exception of one: a striking cobalt-blue tangerine offset to the left of center. The words *"La Mandarine Bleue"* were printed in an arch over the top.

Pointing to it, Zoe said decisively, "That's it; that's the one."

Sally smiled and said, "That's my favorite too. I'll put them to a vote at our next meeting."

Everyone was excited by the unexpected call from Larry to gather at Bill and Zoe's home a few days earlier than they had originally planned to meet. Their potential chefs were traveling through Boise on their way back to Coeur d'Alene from a cooking event in San Francisco, so Larry scheduled an impromptu meeting where everyone could meet the pair.

As the guests stepped through the massive doors of Bill and Zoe's lovely home on Harrison Boulevard, the scintillating aroma of tarragon and thyme flirted shamelessly with their olfactory receptors. It was like stepping through the gates of Heaven.

Hands in motion, Dwayne was elated to share that Larry was in *his* version of paradise helping prep for chef Élise and her pastry chef husband, Henri. In Dwayne's excitement, he made each word a complete sentence. "You. Are. *Not!* Going. To. Believe. The. Menu." All he lacked was a baton to mirror a maestro in the emotional throes of conducting an orchestra.

Bill interjected to say that instead of eating in the kitchen, they'd enjoy their meal in the formal dining room. Before disappearing, Dwayne said, "I paired the wines and am helping Larry serve. You'll get to meet Élise and Henri," which he carefully pronounced 'on-ree.'

Once seated at the massive table, speculation about the menu began. "I'm sure I smell seafood," Sally whispered. Peter nodded in agreement and looked to Zoe for her guess. She raised her eyebrow and smiled coyly before admitting to having peeked into the kitchen. "In my defense, it *is* my kitchen after all."

Bright-eyed and eager to share the delights to come, Larry and Dwayne entered to announce the menu and wines. Larry started, "We're launching this evening with *Escargot Beignet*. Buttered snails, shiitake mushrooms, bacon, and onions, sauce *bourguignonne*."

Dwayne picked up, "I've paired that with a rustic, earthy, and acidic Pinot Noir from the Burgundy wine region in France."

"Served with fresh baguettes, the salad this evening," Larry continued, "is *Salade avec Laitue*. It's comprised of arugula and bibb lettuces, tarragon, chervil, and chives drizzled with a lemon, sweet vermouth, and black pepper vinaigrette."

Dwayne added, "I've paired that with a Tibouren rosé from Provence."

Larry continued, "That delight will be followed by grilled monkfish, tuna, and lobster *bouillabaisse* with tomatoes, fennel, and saffron in a citrus butter sauce."

To which Dwayne added, "I've paired that with a particularly dry Chenin Blanc from the Loire Valley of France."

Peter beamed and tipped his glass in Dwayne's direction.

"We'll eat dessert later when you meet Élise and Henri. Suffice it to say that it's to die for," he finished.

And with that, Larry and Dwayne turned on their heels and went back to the kitchen.

The blue and white chalk stripe aprons both men wore hadn't been lost on anyone. Overseeing the restaurant's decor, Amina said, "The split-front **bistro** apron is one of my favorites. When Yousef and I were doing our research, we decided on this shin-length apron's sleek, clean look and full coverage."

Yousef added, "When I tried one on, my favorite parts were the large front pocket and the center divider for easy movement. Another winning factor is that it's perfect for either front or back of house."

After the first course was served, Bill said, "I'd like to propose a toast. *La Mandarine Bleue* is now part of the National Restaurant Association." Everyone around the table smiled and raised their glasses. *"A bientôt*—cheers!"

If it wasn't bad form, they would have licked their plates clean. "Whoever said sex is better than food obviously hasn't tasted *this* food," Sally announced with a cheeky grin.

Excusing himself, Bill said, "Let me check to see if it's safe to carry our plates into the kitchen to meet the creators of this evening's excellent meal. I'll be right back."

Returning momentarily with a smile on his face he said, "Gather your tableware and follow me." Once everything had been set on an empty counter, they gave Élise, Henri, Larry, and Dwayne a standing ovation. Clearly pleased, the four of them bowed at the waist and accepted the well-earned compliment.

Zoe suggested, "Everyone, grab a seat around the island so we can meet and get to know Élise and Henry."

The kitchen erupted in rapid-fire conversation. Larry and Dwayne explained that they'd already given a tour of *La Mandarine Bleue*, bare as it was, to Élise and Henri and had shared the plans for the kitchen and dining area with them. Élise and Henri were impressed and said they'd like to be part of something from the ground up; they'd not had an opportunity like that before.

The group learned that the couple, originally from Provence, France, met in Paris when they'd trained at *Le Cordon Bleu*: Élise in the cuisine training program, Henri in pastry. Their notable experience backed by impressive letters of recommendation made them a tempting package deal. Their combined competencies would add sought-after expertise to Boise's food scene. It would also come with a price tag to match.

Clearing his throat, Henri said, "Let us clean up the kitchen while you talk in private. I've made a simple pear *clafoutis* you can enjoy with *café* over your discussion."

"*Well*?" asked Larry and Dwayne. Their eager faces made them look like proud parents of the pair.

"In for a penny, in for a pound," said Sally.

"We agree," nodded Yousef and Amina.

"If we're going to do this, we might as well do it right," Sheila said as Peter nodded his enthusiastic agreement, his mouth too full to speak.

"Who knows? We may even earn a Michelin star!" agreed Zoe. Bill nodded, his mouth also full.

Back in the kitchen, their decision announced, the sound of celebration echoed as champagne corks flew.

Course Seven—*Rôti*

Pronounced "row-dee," this is the roasted meat course.

. . . .

Rôti de Porc Poêlé avec Sauce Moutarde à la Normande—**Roast Pork with Mustard Sauce**
Serves 6

Ingredients
- 1 cup dry white wine
- 6 garlic cloves, pressed
- ¼ cup olive oil
- 2 tablespoons coarsely chopped fresh rosemary
- 1 tablespoon coarsely chopped fresh thyme
- 8 whole allspice, crushed
- 2 (12-ounce) pork tenderloins
- 5 tablespoons dijon mustard, divided
- ¾ cup heavy cream
- ½ cup low-salt chicken broth
- 2 tablespoons chopped fresh tarragon

Preparation
Mix wine, garlic, oil, rosemary, thyme, and allspice in a large resealable plastic bag. Add pork and turn to coat.

Marinate at least 30 minutes and up to 1 hour, turning bag occasionally.

Preheat oven to 375°F. Remove pork from marinade and place on rack on rimmed baking sheet. Discard marinade. Spread 3 tablespoons mustard all over pork. Roast until thermometer inserted into thickest part of pork registers 145°F, about 25 minutes. Transfer pork to a platter and let stand 10 minutes.

Meanwhile, boil cream, broth, tarragon, and remaining 2 tablespoons mustard in heavy medium saucepan until reduced to 1 cup, whisking occasionally for about 10 minutes. Season sauce to taste with pepper.

Slice pork crosswise into rounds and serve with sauce.

Pairing Note

Enjoy this course with Grenache, a red wine produced in regions all over the world including Côtes du Rhone, France.

Lay Your Cards on the Table

"Style, I think, is *panache*. Who are you? What did you do today? And what are you worth to me? What do you have to offer the world? How did you spend your time today on this planet? How are you spending your time every second? What are you doing now? Are you alive, or are you somnambulant?"

—**TOM HARDY,** actor and producer

For a moment, think of yourself as a business. In our personal lives, defining our personal value—what we're excited about, what we excel at, what comes naturally to us—is the counterpart of defining a business offering in the business arena. There's likely to be value-overlap in our business and personal lives.

In the business arena, we present our value in the form of a résumé, account of work experience, qualifications, and skills we bring to the workplace. Program director and master of strategic communication at Westminster College, Curtis Newbold tells us, "The good résumé is the one that perfectly adapts design and content to an employer's expectations, personal tastes, and goals and highlights all the skills necessary for the position, plus does a little something extra to 'wow' the employer."[3]

When crafting a resume:

- ○ *Set a target.* Aim for businesses that need what you have to offer.
- ○ *Identify strengths.* Articulate what you know, what you can do.
- ○ *Tie strengths to a target position.* Show why you're the person to hire.
- ○ *Provide evidence.* Cite measurable achievements (evidence of your strengths).

Here are examples of business strengths. Notice the word "I" isn't used. Instead, each bullet point starts with a descriptor that's never used twice:

- ○ Exemplary written and oral communication skills—clear, concise, articulate
- ○ Engaging presentation style—interactive, diplomatic, persuasive
- ○ Superior interpersonal skills—team player/builder, conflict resolver
- ○ Flexible in fast-paced situations with emerging and changing requirements
- ○ Strong people skills—approachable, excellent listener, empathetic
- ○ Ability to establish priorities in the face of competing demands
- ○ Views high quality as a vital standard, pays close attention to detail
- ○ Excellent time management skills—self-motivated, proactive, resourceful
- ○ Delivers excellent customer service—solution-oriented, invigorated by personal interaction
- ○ Thrives in both independent and collaborative work environments

○ Enjoys learning—quickly grasps and assimilates fresh ideas and new technology

"You are not your résumé, you are your work."

—**SETH GODIN**, entrepreneur, marketer, public speaker, and author

In our personal lives, what's the value we add to our family, friends, and neighbors? Why should they remain in our sphere of influence? What do we have to offer? What are our ethics?

1. Are you reliable; can others depend on you?
2. Are you honest; do you tell the truth?
3. Are you optimistic; do you encourage others?
4. Are you respectable; do you respect others?
5. Are you hopeful; do you help others see the light at the end of the tunnel?
6. Are you fun to be around; do you have a sense of humor?
7. Are you kind and compassionate; do you lend a helping hand?
8. Are you flexible; do you try different things?
9. Are you inclusive; do you accept and celebrate others?
10. Are you peaceful; do you work toward unity?
11. Are you modest; do you point to the accomplishments of others?
12. Are you enthusiastic; do you share a contagious zest?
13. Are you patient; do you take delays in stride?
14. Are you cooperative; do you work well with others?
15. Are you tactful; do you have a gracious way of communicating?
16. Are you forgiving; do you let go of grudges?
17. Are you resilient; do you bounce back and help others do the same?
18. Are you a visionary; do you leverage imagination, inspiration, and creativity?

19. Are you grateful; do you show gratitude?
20. Are you loyal; do you stay true to those in your sphere of influence?
21. Are you perseverant; do you continue despite opposition?
22. Are you wise; do you integrate the wisdom you have with the life that you live?

Each of the above-listed virtues is a personal choice that can be intentionally nurtured and cultivated.

After the 2016 presidential election, someone asked me, "What action steps are you taking to help our nation heal and to live your beliefs?"

In 2017 I chose *sankalpa* to be my focus world. *Sankalpa* is a Sanskrit word that means determination, a practical step to harness willpower. With this resolve, I'm liberally planting, cultivating, and nurturing seeds of:

○ *Hope*—optimism, joyful expectation
○ *Grace*—the immediate presence of spirit, be the change
○ *Peace*—reconciliation, unity

My practical and ideological steps to ensure a good harvest include exercising intentional kindness. To build up, not tear down. To unite, not divide. To celebrate differences, not merely accept or tolerate them. To be better informed. To be transparent and vulnerable, not guarded and closed. And to actively listen, not passively hear what people with opposing viewpoints have to share.

What seeds are you planting?

"Who sows virtue reaps honor."

—**LEONARDO DA VINCI,** artist, architect, and inventor

Inner Alchemy

One of the things that can have the greatest impact on our internal landscape is sorrow. It doesn't discriminate; it's non-biased. Transcending all differences, it affects people of every age, gender, sexual orientation, ethnicity, culture, education, socioeconomic status, spiritual tradition, culture, and political stance. It's part of the human experience; no one is immune.

Sorrow is born from loss. Its razor-sharp blade cuts to the heart—the seat of our emotions—whether we've lost our job, our home, our health, an opportunity, or a loved one.

Some of the world's most beautiful artwork and literature comes from deep places of pain and suffering. But prolonged or unrelenting sorrow—despair and hopelessness—can destroy.

Happiness is a feeling. It fluctuates based on external circumstances. It's temporary, fleeting at best. For instance, we check the mailbox and find a notice from the IRS informing us that we owe a considerable sum in back taxes. For most people, our happiness level would plunge.

On the flip side, we check the mailbox and find an unexpected refund check and our happiness level soars.

Happiness can also be a result of manufactured merriment such as going to the circus, watching a funny movie, or attending a party.

Different than happiness, when our perspective—the lens through which we view life—is governed from the inside out, the external pressures fall away, and we experience joy.

Joy is a state of being. It's inexplicable peace even in the midst of turmoil. Joy is internal, and when nurtured and encouraged, it becomes resident—abiding—regardless of external circumstances.

There are people who suffer tremendous personal devastation yet retain a state of joy—inexplicable peace. Viktor Frankl is a perfect example. As a Viennese Jew, he was interned by the Germans for more than three years, but being confined by the narrow boundaries of a concentration camp didn't rob him of joy. In his book *Man's Search for Meaning*, he wrote, "In some way, suffering ceases to be suffering at the moment it finds a meaning, such as the meaning of a sacrifice."

Joy is our inner response to meaning—to hope. Cultivating and maintaining our inner garden eases the struggle that exists along life's path, and with the passage of time, sorrow can amazingly transform into colorful blooms of love, forgiveness, humor, contentment, gratitude, and a renewed sense of purpose.

"If our hearts are ready for anything, we can open to our inevitable losses, and to the depths of our sorrow. We can grieve our lost loves, our lost youth, our lost health, our lost capacities. This is part of our humanness, part of the expression of our love for life."

—**TARA BRACH,** psychologist, teacher, and author

SECTION EIGHT

Market Positioning and Stategy

La Mandarine Bleue

Course Eight—*Légume*

Do You See What I See?

Market Positioning and Strategy

"In marketing, I've seen only one strategy that can't miss—
and that is to market to your best customers first, your best
prospects second, and the rest of the world last."

—**JOHN ROMERO,** director, designer, programmer, and
developer in the video game industry

In today's message-heavy consumer arena, it's imperative
that marketing hit the bullseye as soon as it's experienced by our ideal
customer. That's where market positioning and strategy come into play;
it's a way for brands to penetrate the advertising chaos and impress
consumers they have a chance of influencing.

Market positioning was introduced in 1969 by Jack Trout and Al
Ries. In their book *Positioning: The Battle for Your Mind*, market positioning is described as "an organized system for finding a window in the
customer's mind, based on the idea that communication can only take
place at the right time and under the right circumstances."

Simplicity is key. But simple doesn't mean easy. It takes confidence,
determination, and follow-through.

A statement of market positioning looks like this when broken
down into steps:

1. *Positioning statement.* The statement should answer the
   following questions: What's your brand and what does it

stand for? Who are your target consumers, and what do they need? How will you meet their needs? Who is the competition, and what do they do differently?

2. *Identify your uniqueness.* What's the difference between your communication channel and the competition's?

3. *Competitor analysis.* How do your strengths and weaknesses measure up against theirs?

4. *Current position.* You must know your market position to compete for your share.

5. *Competitor position.* How much power can your competitor flex in the marketplace?

6. *Unique positioning.* A formal statement of who you are, who you're not, and who your best target is.

7. *Test.* Leveraging data gathered from the previous steps, test your newly-formulated brand positioning concept. This may involve surveys, focus groups, polls, **ethnography**, and interviews.

Sam Walton, the founder of WalMart, didn't operate a store better than anyone else. What set him apart—took him from cutting edge to bleeding edge—was the successful retail strategy he developed.

When your product or service is similar to their product or service, your care, skill, and strategy are critical. Who, exactly, do you serve? Your model, costs, and benefits must be different. Just because you're used to the strategy you use now, doesn't mean it'll always serve you well.

McDonald's is a perfect example of changing with the times. In his *Forbes* article "Starbucks and McDonald's Winning Strategy," business and investment strategist Panos Mourkoukoutas says, "In the 1960s McDonald's rode the baby-boomer trend, supplying fast and inexpensive food to the burgeoning teenage population and ever-increasing female labor force.

"Through the 1970s and 1980s, McDonald's established golden arches—'The American Way of Life'—in countries around the globe by franchising to locals.

"In the 1990s and early 2000s, McDonald's revamped its image by refurbishing and updating their restaurants to a more natural dining environment, supplementing the fast and convenient elements with healthier components such as carrot sticks, fruits, and salads.

"McDonald's continues to expand offerings in their traditional restaurants and Cafés with specialty coffees and healthy drinks that compete with Starbucks.

"Because of their savvy franchise business model—collective entrepreneurship where everyone shares in the risks and rewards—McDonald's has become the standard for other franchise organizations to model themselves after."[2]

Bippity Boppity Boo

Repeat business is dependent on the customer's experience, on their perception of their interaction with any and every part of an organization. In turn, their view affects behaviors and builds memories, which drive customer loyalty and affects the economic value an organization generates. In other words, customer experience is everything.

In their book *The Intuitive Customer: 7 Imperatives for Moving Your Customer Experience to the Next Level,* authors Colin Shaw and Ryan Hamilton explain that "many businesses focus on the rational aspects of the customer experience—price, for example, or room size, or whether the menu includes both steak and seafood. But customers are not rational! They mostly make irrational decisions based on emotions and past experiences.

"The key to a successful customer experience is to embrace customers' irrational nature and commit to understanding customer's habits and behaviors. Customers make a lot of decisions based on intuition and habit because it's easy. Processing rational information like price and quality is harder, and so—especially when they're feeling stressed or lazy—customers buy based on intuition and then come up with a rational justification later."

We would all do well to take a page from Carnival Corporation's new Ocean Medallion Technology, a wearable device that's set to debut on the Regal Princess cruise ship in 2017 and anticipate their customers' desire, sometimes even before they do.

In Colin Shaw's case study "Enhance your CX With This Technology" he explains the Ocean Medallion technology: "Each passenger will receive a personalized token that can be worn around your neck, on your wrist, or carried in your pocket. The token interacts with 7,000 sensors through the ship to track where you are and what you're doing. And it uses that information to predict what you'd like to do next. The sensors interact with 4,000 high-resolution screens through the ship to provide personalized recommendations.

"For example, if you took a Zumba class yesterday, you might like yoga today. If you ordered a mid-afternoon cocktail, perhaps you'd like another. The sensors go beyond making recommendations and use technology to ensure that passengers are always comfortable, even turning on lights and adjusting room temperature as guests walk toward their rooms."

Shaw explains, "The Ocean Medallion technology follows on the heels of Disney's 'MagicBand' and a similar device on Royal Caribbean cruises, but it goes even farther in predicting and responding to customer needs and desires."[3] Now *that's* a customer focused organization!

Minding the Gap

Market positioning and strategy begs the question, "How do you see your customers?" And even more important, "How do your customers see you?"

Thanks to technology, the transient nature of customers has increased significantly. Because of this, retail and other **business to business** industries have to be more focused than ever on delivering an exceptional customer experience: from marketing and sales to implementation and customer support. And the opportunity for a gap to occur between the client and the product has increased as well.

When I was in the corporate world one of the jaw-dropping events that occurred all too often was the sales team promising deliverables that either (a) couldn't be accomplished in the timeframe they'd guaranteed the client or (b) committed to a product that wasn't possible for the implementation team to design or execute—not in this lifetime.

Unfortunately, unfounded guarantees quickly widen the space between customer and company. It can grow from gap to chasm in a heartbeat. Not only with an external client but with internal team members.

Documented success criteria that everyone understands and agrees to is imperative and helps mind the gap.

It's a team effort. Instead of the sales team moving on to the next deal, they would do well to remain involved with the account to help mediate and clarify. By understanding exactly what it takes to implement the solution they're selling, it can be delivered on time and under budget, or on budget and ahead of schedule. Either way, the client is happy.

Further, the customer retains warm and fuzzy feelings when the "go live" is handled seamlessly and they don't see or feel a handoff from the implementation team to the support team. Just like sales people stay with the implementation team during a well-designed transition, the implementation team should stay with the support team during that transition.

The common denominator in all exceptional customer experiences is that the customer's trust never falters.

> "What we need to do is always lean into the future; when the world changes around you and when it changes against you—what used to be a tail wind is now a head wind—you have to lean into that and figure out what to do because complaining isn't a strategy."
>
> —**JEFF BEZOS,** founder, chairman, and CEO of Amazon.com

La Mandarine Bleue

"Cooking is like painting or writing a song. Just as there are only so many notes or colors, there are only so many flavors—it's how you combine them that sets you apart."

—**WOLFGANG PUCK,** celebrity chef, restauranteur, and cookbook author

Arms loaded with their various works in progress, everyone arrived at Amina and Yousef's bungalow in the North End. Everyone, that is, except for Bill who, much like a traffic cop—all he needed were gloves and a whistle—was overseeing a collaborative effort at *La Mandarine Bleue*. Humming with activity, an assembly of tradespeople occupied the space: plumbers, electricians, carpenters.

Shifting roles from traffic cop to referee, Bill joined the painter and floor installer who were taking measurements and debating on whose work should be done first.

"I should paint first, so I don't have to be careful of your floors," the painting contractor said.

"I should install the flooring first, so I don't have to be careful of your newly painted walls," the flooring contractor countered.

Bill looked directly at the flooring contractor and stated, "Here's what we're going to do. Once the plumber, electrician, and carpenter finish, the current floor will be removed along with any remaining debris. We've hired a post-construction cleaning service to eliminate all of the dust, dirt, and grime once it's gone."

Turning to the painting contractor, he continued, "The painting will be next," then shifting his gaze back to the flooring contractor he said, "followed by the flooring and baseboards once the paint is bone dry. And gentlemen, I do appreciate your cooperation." He finished with a meaningful look at them both.

Smiling at the group assembled in her living room, Amina said, "We're going to start with food in the hopes that Bill makes it in time for the business portion, or at least most of it. I'll keep a plate warm for him."

Yousef picked up, "We made one of the potential menu recipes Larry gave us. Please serve yourself in the kitchen, then bring your plates back here." He motioned for them to follow as he led the way. And while the fragrant scent that greeted them from the steaming pot on the stove bespoke France, the ambience of the kitchen visually transported the group to the culture, color, and natural beauty of Morocco. Welcomed by Mediterranean-blue, sunshine-yellow, and olive-leaf-green patterned tiles, it was easy to picture themselves in a spice souk in Marrakech.

Each person dished smoked salmon and asparagus salad onto their plates while Amina ladled helpings of *boeuf bourguignon*—a traditional French stew of beef braised in red wine with carrots and mushrooms—into deep cardamom-colored bowls with buttered noodles at the bottom. Originally a peasant meal, this aromatic stew is now a staple of French haute cuisine.

Yousef enthusiastically pulled large hunks of bread from a crusty French loaf and placed one on each salad plate as his guests left the kitchen and headed to the living room to sit on plump pillows and Moroccan leather poufs situated around a large, low-set table.

Bearing wine and glasses, Amina and Yousef joined the others in the throes of food ecstasy. They were greeted by a simultaneous chorus of "Fantastic!" "*Délicieux!*" "*Exquisité!*" "Delectable!"

"I'm glad you're enjoying it," Amina said while pouring ample helpings of Pinot Noir into wine glasses. Raising her glass, she said, "*À l'inspecteur de la santé*—to the health inspector. If I'm not mistaken, he's visiting *La Mandarine Bleue* soon."

A unanimous "*À l'inspecteur de la santé. A bientôt!*" sounded in the living room as they continued enjoying their feast.

Zoe announced, "I'm excited to share that our chefs have given their notice at the restaurant in Coeur d'Alene and when they arrive in Boise they're going to stay in our guest house while they house hunt."

Just as they were about to start the business meeting, Bill arrived. "I'm sorry I'm late. Gosh but it smells good in here!"

"I've saved a plate for you. Have a seat, and we'll be right back." She and Yousef took the opportunity to gather the empty dishes and took them to the kitchen. They returned with a steaming bowl and crisp salad for their famished friend.

"While Bill catches up with the rest of us who've already stuffed ourselves, Zoe and I will bring everyone up to speed on where we're at. Zoe, you start," said Sally gesturing toward her.

"With a customer first perspective, I've set up Facebook, Twitter, and Instagram accounts for *La Mandarine Bleue*. And while they're not quite finished, I'm in the process of establishing our presence on Yelp and TripAdvisor. Once those are set, I'll send one email with all of the links to everyone so you can have a look. And by the way, our logo looks great on the internet!" To everyone's delight, she ended her update by placing fingers to lips, and with a kiss and flip of her wrist, offered an inspired and enthusiastic, "*Très magnifique!*"

Sheila added brightly, "Once I receive the links for the accounts Zoe set up, I'll add those and our LinkedIn and Pinterest logos to the social media area of our website. As Zoe said, our perspective is customer first, and it shows in our web presence."

"I feel like a dinosaur," Bill said. "Could you please help me understand what those logos on the *La Mandarine Bleue* website do? All of those words—Facebook, Twitter, Instagram, Yelp, TripAdvisor, LinkedIn, Pinterest—sound like a foreign language to me."

"Absolutely," Sally answered. "Each one represents a social media venue that has unique advantages for sharing blog posts, tips and techniques, branded images, and other content that appeals to our target audience. And to help manage it, we'll use a product called Hootsuite to schedule posts and Tweetdeck for monitoring Twitter activity."

Bill smiled and shook his head.

Dwayne jumped in, "I've offered to write a short blog post every other week, and Larry will post a recipe on the in-between weeks."

Larry continued, "To subscribe to our blog and receive recipes, people have to give us their email address. Those addresses will help us grow our mailing list. And we can use MailChimp to help us manage that," he finished smiling.

Bemused, Bill laughed and said, "Hootsuite, Tweetdeck, and MailChimp. I'll stick with spreadsheets thank you very much!"

Amina and Yousef who'd slipped out momentarily returned. Yousef carried a tray of cups and rich-smelling *café*, Amina held another that held a plate mounded with *Madeleines* (French tea cookies) for dipping into the fondue pot of melted dark chocolate next to it. Placing them on the table, she invited, "Please, help yourselves."

After a melt-in-your-mouth bite, Larry exclaimed, "These are wonderful!" The rest of the group nodded in agreement, their mouths too full to speak.

After a sip of *café*, Sheila said, "The thirty-six-inch *maître d'* station podium is scheduled to arrive at the end of this week. With our customer-first perspective in mind, we also have reservation software loaded on the front of house computer for people who reserved online or called the restaurant directly—either way. That's the same computer that's tied to the cash register where our point of sale system accepts all major credit cards." Looking at Bill with a smile, she added, "And it's interfaced with the accounting software you requested."

Peter said, "All of the glassware will arrive before our pre-opening event. Once the new floor is in, we'll receive all the wine we've ordered from our distributor, and our liquor license becomes active opening day."

Looking at Bill, Yousef asked, "Speaking of new floors, did you talk with the contractors today?"

"Yes, I did," Bill said.

"Perfect," Yousef smiled. "The electrician has started installing the lighting, and the sound system is next. The French-inspired playlist is push-button ready, and Amina and I have selected several pieces of artwork for you to choose from once the dining area is painted and the tables are in and dressed."

Amina said, "The white restaurant tablecloths and napkins will arrive this week. We've subscribed to a local laundry service that will take care of the aprons and chef's wear as well. The flatware arrives next week and so does the tableware. It's white with a striking, cobalt-blue pinstripe around the edge."

Hands over his now-full stomach, Bill contemplatively said, "This is wonderful. Our love of excellent cuisine was what brought us together, and now we're looking to provide a superb dining experience to our customers. Instead of viewing things from owners' perspectives, we're making decisions as if we're the guests. Hopefully, we'll exceed their expectations with all our customer-first planning and they'll come back for more." He looked up and with a smile and raised eyebrow added, "After telling others about La Mandarine Bleue, of course."

Course Eight—*Légume*

Pronounced **"lay-gume,"** this is the vegetable course.

. . . .

Flageolet Beans—these French beans are known as "the caviar of beans"

Serves 6-8

Ingredients
- 1 pound dried flageolet beans
- 2 tablespoons good olive oil
- 4 ounces bacon, diced
- 2 cups medium-diced yellow onion (2 onions)
- 2 cups medium-diced fennel, trimmed and cored
- 2 carrots, scrubbed and medium-diced
- 4 teaspoons minced garlic (4 cloves)
- 2 cups canned beef or vegetable broth
- 2 bay leaves
- 1 large sprig fresh rosemary
- Kosher salt and freshly ground black pepper

Preparation
The night before cooking, place the beans in a large bowl and cover them with water by 1 inch. Cover the bowl with plastic wrap and refrigerate overnight.

The next day, preheat the oven to 300°F. Drain the beans, rinse well, and drain again. In a large ovenproof pot such as Le Creuset, heat the olive oil over medium to medium-low heat. Add the bacon, and cook for 4 to 5 minutes until the bacon starts to brown. Add the onion, fennel, and carrots and cook for 7 minutes, stirring occasionally until the vegetables begin to soften but aren't browned. Add the garlic and sauté for 1 to 2 more minutes.

Add the flageolets to the pot and stir in the broth, bay leaves, and rosemary. *Don't be tempted to add salt! The beans will become tough.*

Add 2 cups of water, which should just cover the beans, and bring to a simmer on top of the stove. Cover the pot tightly and bake in the oven for 45 minutes. Remove the lid, stir in 1 tablespoon salt and 1 teaspoon pepper, and return the pot to the oven without the lid. Raise the temperature to 350°F and bake for 30 to 45 more minutes. The beans will be tender, and there will be just a little liquid in the bottom of the pan. If the beans are dry, add a little more water.

Discard the bay leaves and rosemary. Taste for seasoning and serve hot.

Pairing Note

Enjoy this course with Chardonnay, a white wine originally produced in the Burgundy wine region of eastern France but now grown wherever wine is produced.

Do You See What I See?

"It's not only moving that creates new starting points. Sometimes all it takes is a subtle shift in perspective, an opening of the mind, an intentional pause and reset, or a new route to start to see new options and new possibilities."

—**KRISTIN ARMSTRONG,** professional road bicycle racer, and three-time Olympic gold medalist

For a moment, think of yourself as a business. In our personal lives, perspective is the counterpart of market positioning and strategy in the business arena.

One day, at the end of each of my client sessions, I asked the question "What is life?" I received the following responses:

"Life is our chance to be useful, to make a positive difference."

"Life is nothing but the echo of joy disappearing into the great chasm of misery."

"Life is people looking for similarly broken people. We communicate through damage."

"Life is a single skip for joy."

The same question garnered four completely different responses.

When I go to a gallery to enjoy artwork, I find that I don't stand still in front of a piece. I pivot; I move around and view it from many different angles. I shift my perspective. French novelist, Marcel Proust said,

"The voyage of discovery is not seeking new landscapes, but in having new eyes." A shift in perspective is just that.

Have you ever experienced a noticeable emotional reaction to someone? That response can be due to a reflection of a beautiful aspect of our personal essence, or it can be recognition of a shadow—ours. When I find myself judging a person, place, or thing, I make a point to move—mentally or physically—so I can observe from a different angle. I shift my perspective.

Meditation (quiet contemplation) is driven by our point of view—how we see things. These thoughts shape our lives. As written in the Talmud, "We don't see things as they are; we see them as we are." Individually and collectively our thoughts contribute to the healing, or the demise, of the planet.

In my experience, shifting one's mental outlook (perspective) even slightly can significantly change the view and reveal that the sun is coming up beyond the dark horizon. Oprah Winfrey is an excellent example of this. She said, "Anything can be a miracle, a blessing, an opportunity if you choose to see it that way. Had I not been demoted from my six o'clock anchor position in Baltimore back in 1977, the talk show gig would have never happened when it did."[4]

In *Shift Into Thrive: Six Strategies for Women to Unlock the Power of Resiliency*, authors Lynn Schmidt, PhD and Kevin Nourse, PhD observe that "the perspective of Oprah in reframing adversity to an opportunity is the essence of resiliency."

They go on to explain: "Resilient people learn from their challenges, make choices about their future, and take deliberate action to move forward. Rather than merely waiting for tough times to happen, resilient people anticipate adversity and prepare for it. When faced with adversity, these individuals experience a less dramatic downturn in their functioning and are less likely to get trapped in the negative emotions they experience."

My brick and mortar facility had two treatment rooms and a small store with wellness offerings. At the end of each year, I asked myself, "What do I need to *add* to HolEssence to make it even better?"

One year, I reframed the question and instead asked, "What do I need to *subtract* from HolEssence to make it even better?" In my case, it was the product. I hosted a large sales event to eliminate all of it from inventory. This decision allowed me to showcase something I already had in stock: space, lots of space, that I rented to a variety of holistic health practitioners (i.e., yoga, massage, acupuncture), and I started offering a variety of classes.

A successful business move, this shift in perspective had a tremendous, positive effect in that I had an income stream without product overhead. And while changing from product to a service offering may not be right for you, there are other options to consider:

- From storefront to the web
- From invitation only to everyone is welcome
- From mass production to custom
- From restaurant venue to catering or vice versa

Another valuable shift in perspective is to examine the habits of your favorite entrepreneurs and note the things they *don't* do. In his article "6 Things Great Entrepreneurs Don't Do That Set Them Apart From The Mediocre" Ryan Westwood, CEO of Simplus observed:

- They don't watch their email.
- They don't attend too many meetings.
- They don't get too busy to think.
- They don't try to provide too many products or services.
- They don't micromanage.
- They don't outgrow the need for a mentor.

Unfortunately, mentor relationships aren't pursued often enough. Growth marketer and entrepreneur Sujan Patel says, "A lot of people fail to recognize the true value of having someone to talk to or confide in, and it's a real shame because mentoring matters. It makes a difference, and it can impact your business in very tangible ways."[5]

Inside Looking

In 2014 I learned about the Japanese form of self-reflection known as *Naikan* (pronounced "nye-con"), which translates to "inside looking." This practice is a shift in perspective from dwelling on a past or present conflict to instead focus on the care and support we've received in our lives. It inspires us to accept life's events instead of becoming bogged down in our feelings about them.

One of the leading authorities on Naikan in the United States, Gregg Krech and his wife, Linda, founded and operate the TóDó Institute in Monkton, Vermont, a nonprofit center that offers educational programs on Japanese psychology, including Naikan; the emphasis on which is daily practice in order to weave the skill into the tapestry of one's life.

In an interview with Angela Winter for *The Sun* titled "Many Thanks: Gregg Krech On The Revolutionary Practice of Gratitude," Krech said, "The practice of Naikan is based on three questions:

1. What have I received from (person's name)?
2. What have I given to (same person's name)?
3. What troubles and difficulties have I caused (same person's name)?"

He goes on to explain, "These questions provide a foundation for reflecting on relationships with others such as parents, friends, teachers, siblings, work associates, children, spouses, and partners. In each case, we search for a more realistic view of our conduct and of the give and take which has occurred in the relationship."

During the interview, Krech told Angela Winter, "People have a keen interest in asking a fourth question: 'What troubles and difficulties have this person caused me?' but in the practice of Naikon, it's important to stay on track. For individuals who criticize and complain about other people, it's a big change, but once they understand the framework, it can be helpful or even healing."

The premise being that as we list what we've received from another person we're grounded in the simple reality of how we've been supported and cared for. Some people gain a deeper sense of gratitude and appreciation.

Next in the practice we look at the other side of the equation: "What have I given to the other person?" "What troubles and difficulties have I caused them?" In her interview with Krech, Angela Winter learned that there's something transformational about looking honestly at the way in which we've caused suffering, the ways in which we've hurt people.

Naikan is life research. We collect and analyze data and then draw a conclusion. Many people conclude they've received much more than they've given, both to individual people and to the world in general. It can mean the difference between seeing life as an entitlement and seeing it as a gift.

In the practice of Naikon we learn that "Without a conscious shift in perspective to the myriad ways in which the world supports us, we risk our attention being trapped by problems and obstacles, leaving us to linger in self-pity."[6]

"Miracles happen everyday, change your perception of what a miracle is and you'll see them all around you."

—JON BON JOVI, singer-songwriter, record producer,
philanthropist

SECTION NINE

Marketing and Selling Model

La Mandarine Bleue

Course Nine—*Entremet*

Sis Boom Bah!

Marketing and Selling Model

"If you have integrity, nothing else matters. If you don't have integrity, nothing else matters."

—**HARVEY MACKAY,** businessman, syndicated columnist, and author

Resting squarely on the shoulders of the sales force, the marketing and selling model is where the rubber meets the road.

Top sales performers exhibit the leadership talent of self-confidence with disciplined consistency. If they don't believe in themselves, how can they inspire confidence in others—specifically their prospects?

Sometimes people use the terms self-esteem and self-confidence interchangeably, but they're vastly different.

Self-esteem is our sense of worth. It's acknowledging and respecting our personal value—who we are and what we do. It recognizes inaccurate messages that can permeate our consciousness. It's being diligent about authenticating the truth, or non-truth, behind the messages.

When our self-esteem is healthy, we feel lovable and capable. This, in part, is gleaned from those around us (being loved and valued) and earned (becoming a capable, growing person). Both components are equally important.

When we don't have self-esteem, we feel unworthy. Unworthiness stems from complex negative memories and emotions.

Self-confidence isn't arrogance that's often associated with over-confidence; it's an assured, self-possession, something that allows us to move forward with dignity, poise, and grace.

Self-confidence is the personal belief that "I own" what it takes to succeed. People who have this mindset typically have a strong willingness to achieve based on the combination of personal drive (fortitude) and functional (practical) knowledge. They're aware of and embrace their abilities.

Limiting and Empowering Beliefs

Whether religious, spiritual, or personal, beliefs can be either limiting or empowering.

It seems that religion has brought comfort to many people throughout the ages and across the globe. I've seen it give people a sense of a power greater than themselves and provide them with tremendous hope.

Spirituality can be either a part of a specific religion or independent of religion. It can be a self-directed personal inner path—any practice based on a belief in something bigger than ourselves. A person can be religious and not spiritual, or a person can be spiritual and not religious.

In the most basic sense, spirituality is based on the belief that something exists outside the understanding of our five physical senses. It is the desire to attain understanding of, or have a relationship with, the sacred, with what is divine.

Beliefs are something that we embrace—heart and soul. They are something we accept as truth. Beliefs can revolve around ourselves or others and can include things such as faith and identity.

Limiting beliefs are ideas that hold us back, ideas that keep us from becoming the people we want to be or from doing the things we want to do. They're constraining and usually exclusive, not inclusive. Most of the time they aren't even true; they're myths we let control our lives. Many times, we aren't even consciously aware that we have these beliefs. They often exist in our subconscious directing our automatic judgments and influencing our decisions.

If you find yourself saying things like, "I can't," or "There's nothing I can do," or even if you catch yourself using words like *never, always, all,* and *none*, then you probably have some limiting beliefs. If you feel that your life isn't how you want it to be and you feel helpless or hopeless about it, you probably have limiting beliefs.

Empowering beliefs are ideas that launch you forward and help you to become the person you want to be, a person who actively does the things they want to do. When you find yourself harboring a limiting belief ("I can't perform this task," or "I can't fill this role"), think of a replacement belief—one that bathes you in emotions that enhance joy.

Here are some examples of encouraging beliefs:

- I contain unlimited, unleashed potential and possibility.
- I am worthy; I am capable.
- I have enough time for the important things in my life.
- I am the only person responsible for my attitude.
- I have what it takes!

Regardless of the religious tradition, spiritual path, or personal perspective we choose to embrace, the potential exists for it to be positive, uplifting, constructive, and healing. The choice is ours.

Excessive self-confidence quickly becomes self-importance. This often results in a feeling of superiority that can lead to the condescension of others. Having self-confidence without arrogance or an inflated ego can be difficult to maintain.

People with healthy self-confidence are adept at realistic, personal goal setting. As they achieve their goals, it becomes even easier to embrace their ability to be accurate. They're motivated from within; they're self-starters.

Extrinsic rewards such as money and prizes rarely hold appeal for self-starters. Their motivation is internal; it's initiated by the belief that they can face adversity. They adopt positive affirmations—belief statements—that keep them going when others throw in the towel.

Here are some examples:

- I am empowered.
- I am balanced and own my power.
- I act with self-esteem.

- I can handle a crisis.
- I have a strong sense of self.
- I trust my gut instinct.
- I have the courage to take risks.
- I am motivated by confidence.
- I kick butt and take names (in a zen way, of course).

Self-starters populate the sales leadership level of most organizations because of their critical thinking skills—their laser-focus on the desired result—and, because they demonstrate that they can lead themselves first, they show that they can lead others. And because they don't need external supervision or motivation, self-starters are the first people sought by employers in today's highly competitive, global marketplace—a good thing, too, just look at the numbers.

According to the Council of American Survey Research Organizations, US companies spent $6.7 billion in efforts to learn more about their consumers in 2013. Worldwide, $19 billion is invested annually to discover what consumers want.[1] And yet, the marketplace isn't any closer to understanding what motivates consumers to buy what they buy.

Over the last hundred years, at least a dozen marketing models have been used with varying degrees of success.

Below is a sketch of just a few:

- *7 Ps of the Marketing Mix*—product, price, place, promotion, people, process, and physical evidence
- *USP*—Unique Selling Proposition—the concept that brands should make it clear to potential buyers why they're different and better than the competition
- *Customer Lifetime Value Model*—assessing a customer's worth based on the current value of future revenue attributed to a customer's relationship with a product
- *Loyalty Ladder*—the steps a person takes from prospect to loyal brand advocate

This isn't your grandmother's consumer market. With the slew of media options currently available, today's high-tech purchasers buy differently than they did in the past, and what they buy is different too. Further, they can opt out of marketing campaigns in which companies have invested heavily. With the push of a button, they can effectively stop telemarketers, email, and direct mail.

So now what? Today's consumer landscape is larger, more diverse, has more choices, and has a variety of payment options. It's a marketing frontier waiting to be discovered, waiting to be conquered.

In his book *The Science of Why: Decoding Human Motivation and Transforming Marketing Strategy* author David Forbes says, "As our marketplace becomes more and more diverse, changes in the difficulty of researching and attracting our new consumers make understanding what really, deeply motivates them more critical than ever."

Bain & Company is an American global management consulting firm. In an article titled "Is Complexity Killing Your Sales Model?" published in their Insights newsletter they state, "The sales models for many large companies have become more complex and less efficient, putting pressure on profit margins." They attributed this, in part, to four elements:

- ○ Customer needs have grown more sophisticated.
- ○ Customers expect providers to help solve their problems and measure value based on outcomes, not necessarily the lowest price.
- ○ Customers have become more experienced.
- ○ Customers are less loyal because they're wary of being locked into products.

They suggested the following "mutually reinforcing" actions to alleviate the problem:

- ○ Identify customer 'sweet spots' and define the appropriate offering, then put a repeatable process in place to expand to other segments.
- ○ Get the right people and channel—no more, no less—in front of the customer at the right time.
- ○ Design compensation to promote behaviors that support your business goals.

○ Equip the back office to allow sales representatives to spend more time selling."[2]

According to Google BrandLab, a "sweet spot" is "where brands and their audiences intersect."[3]

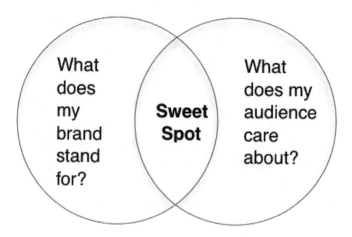

Numbers Don't Lie

In their Harvard Business Review article "New Business Models in Emerging Markets," authors Matthew Eyring, Mark W. Johnson, and Hairi Nair say, "Right now more than 20,000 multinationals are operating in emerging economies. According to the *Economist*, Western multinationals expect to find seventy percent of their future growth there—forty percent of it in China and India alone. But if the opportunity is huge, so are the obstacles to seizing it. On its 2010 Ease of Doing Business Index, the World Bank ranked China 89th, Brazil 129th, and India 133rd out of 183 countries."

Summarizing the bank's conclusions, the *Economist* states, "The only way that companies can prosper in these markets is to cut costs relentlessly and accept profit margins close to zero."[4]

There are just as many sales models as there are marketing models. From personal preparation models to value selling matrix models and everything in between, including presentation-based models and applications models.

In his book *Objection Free Selling: How to Prevent, Preempt, and Respond to Every Sales Objection You Get* Robert DeGroot states that one question is consistent across the board: "What must you believe before you buy something?"

DeGroot continues, "Until human beings change in fundamental psychological ways, they will continue to feel the need to believe certain things (need, value, trust, etc.) about the seller, the product and service, and the benefits they will get when they make the purchase."

"People are most successful when they are in their sweet spot. Your sweet spot is the intersection where your passion meets your greatest strength."

—**KEN COLEMAN,** radio and television sportscaster

La Mandarine Bleue

A question she asks herself daily, "What did you do today to achieve excellence?"

—DELLA GOSSET, executive pastry chef

With the restaurant launch rapidly approaching, time and space seemed to converge at *La Mandarine Bleue*. The painting contractor had done a fantastic job as had the floor installers. Tables, chairs, *maître d'* station podium, linens, tableware, flatware, glassware, pots, pans, and appliances flew in daily like cheerful birds coming home to roost.

One Monday a few weeks before opening, the custom glass lettering on the front door was installed. In addition to the phone number and website address for *La Mandarine Bleue,* potential customers saw their hours at a glance: lunch and dinner served six days a week, brunch on the weekends, closed on Mondays.

Edwards Greenhouse delivered two miniature tangerine trees in glazed, cobalt-blue pots, one for each side of the entry. Upon receipt, Dwayne took meticulous notes regarding their care and well-being. Much like a nervous, first-time parent being reassured by a pediatrician, the delivery person told him that if he had any further questions, all he had to do was call.

On Tuesday, they had a hands-on lesson with the reservation and point-of-sale software salesperson. They had several interviews with potential kitchen and wait staff members that afternoon. The plan was to hire two each for back and front of house.

The building sign and retractable canopy were installed on Wednesday. The cobalt-blue stripes in the awning were in perfect harmony with the blue in their logo. The building inspector was there for the event and gave his hearty approval.

All hands on deck, Thursday was their on-site interview with the *Idaho Statesman* newspaper. They served the journalist and photographer *affogato* with a French twist. A sinfully delicious concoction in which the bottom of a tall glass is lined with praline ice cream and *caramel au beurre salé*, topped with whipped cream and a shot of hot, French espresso. Poured table side, the espresso melts the ice cream, releasing a smoky, campfire scent. Needless to say, the experience wowed the reporters. Smiling, the two left with invitations to the pre-opening event.

The menus arrived on Friday, which would change seasonally. The restaurant's launch would take place in summer. And though they'd each previewed them before being printed, their quiet elegance was even lovelier than they'd imagined:

HORS D'OEUVRES

Assiette de Fruits et Fondue de Brie—wedge of baked brie with ripe melon and berries
Chausson du Fromage de Chèvre—goat cheese tarts
Palourdes au Gratin—baked clams with garlic butter and bread crumbs

SOUPE ET SALADES

Soupe du Jour—ask your server for the chef's soup selection
Soupe a l'Oignon—classic onion soup, made with three types of onions ladled over a slice of baguette covered with melted gruyère
Epinards et Concombres à la Grecque—spinach salad with feta and yogurt garlic dressing
Salade Niçoise—organic greens, flaked tuna, niçoise olives, anchovies, egg, tomatoes, and bell peppers

Salade de Canard—roasted duck with orange sherry vinaigrette, pecans, bacon, and red onions on seasonal greens

SANDWICHES

Fromage au Jambon—roasted ham on gruyère with aioli on a baguette

Poulet—grilled chicken breast with lemon caper sauce, tomato, lettuce, and gruyère on focaccia

Turkey Pesto—thin sliced baked turkey with pickled red onions, lettuce, tomato, and fresh basil pesto on a baguette

Crêpe Saumon Fumé—smoked salmon, pickled red onions, and gruyère melted in a housemade buckwheat crepe

Crêpe Parisian—thin sliced roasted ham and gruyère in a housemade buckwheat crepe

ENTRÉES

Poulet à la Moutarde et au Miel—grilled chicken breast with honey mustard glaze

Champignon Parmentier au Gratin—braised portobello mushrooms, topped with French onion mashed potatoes and gruyère

Pore à la Dijonnaise—sautéed pork tenderloin medallions with an orange compare sauce

Truite Sauté Sauce Amere—sautéed fresh boneless trout with raspberry vinegar butter sauce, tarragon, parsley, and shallots

Brochette d'Agneau a la Greque—lamb brochettes with sweet peppers, zucchini and onions with a Greek citrus sauce of fresh rosemary, orange, lime, and grapefruit juice

Pâtes au Fruits de Mer—bay scallops, prawns, snow peas, and wild mushrooms over egg linguini with a garlic vermouth sauce

Supreme de Volaille—boneless chicken breast sautéed in sherry vinegar butter sauce, with prosciutto and chanterelles

Entrecôte Grille—boneless aged rib-eye with freshly grated horseradish and sauce Bordelaise

DESSERT

Choux à la Crème—chilled cream puffs drizzled with warm chocolate and rum sauce

Crêpes Suzette—fresh crepes with orange, sugar, and flambé in Grand Marnier

Vanille Crème Brûlée aux Framboises—traditional vanilla crème brûlée with fresh raspberries, drizzled with raspberry liqueur sauce

Affogato—praline ice cream drowned in caramel sauce and espresso, topped with whipped cream

Having completed interviews and reference and background checks, on Friday afternoon the owners extended four offers of employment to applicants. Three accepted on the spot. One asked if she could take the weekend to think about it; a junior at Boise State University, she wanted to speak with her parents before accepting.

They also initiated the large commercial dishwashers: one for glassware, the other for everything else. When the kitchen was spotless, Élise and Henri shooed the others out to the dining area and told them to enjoy a glass of wine while the pair whipped up something to appease their appetites.

The group took the opportunity to test the sound system and try every seat in the house. They'd all experienced being seated at a bad table in other restaurants. Yousef had taken pains to avoid guest seating under speakers and the air conditioner, backed up to the front door or the kitchen, too close to the server stations, or where guests could hear receipts printing. The brushed stainless steel double swinging kitchen doors had gravity hinges ensuring silence between front and back of house.

The restrooms were immaculate and would be kept that way. From the beginning, Sally had said, "I judge public places by their restrooms, especially restaurants. If they're not clean and orderly, they don't get my business." They'd also made certain that the women's stalls had a place for coats and purses so nothing would have to touch the floor. The owners made it clear to the front of house staff that they would be responsible for scheduled cleaning and that their pay would be more because they would bear the responsibility for the unpleasant task. They were also aware that Sally would inspect the bathrooms at random, daily.

Élise and Henri entered the dining area bearing trays pre-plated with *Salade Niçoise* and *Truite Sauté Sauce Amere*. Élise said, "We're using the fish market on Vista Avenue on a trial basis. Their fish and seafood is caught in the Pacific and flown in fresh from Seattle every day."

A chorus of "Oh this looks good," "I'm starving," and "It smells divine," went up as the food-laden trays came down and plates were passed around the table. Peter poured wine into glasses for Élise and Henri and proposed a toast to the group, "May we command success by deserving it."

"*A bientôt*—cheers!" went up in unison as they drank to their future.

"Did I hear we have back of house staff coming onboard?" Henri asked the group.

"Yes," Sally answered. "Daniel and Hannah accepted our offers and will be working in the kitchen under your and Élise's direction. I'm sorry the timing didn't work for you to interview them too. They both have kitchen experience. Daniel's been a line cook for three years. He comes from one of the most popular hotel restaurants in Boise. And Hannah has been a prep cook for a year and a half. She comes from a co-op restaurant in Meridian that recently downsized their staff."

Looking to Sheila and Dwayne, Sally continued, "Ethan will work front of house under your direction. We're waiting to hear from Abbie. She said she'd let us know on Monday. They've both waited tables, Ethan at a popular steak and seafood restaurant, Abbie at a country club restaurant. And it just so happens that Abbie speaks French!"

Bill suggested they all pitch in to clear and wash up, reminding everyone, "The double kitchen doors are just like car traffic. Keep to the right when entering the kitchen. Keep to the right when leaving the kitchen. That, along with the windowed doors, will prevent any accidents."

"Unless, of course, you're in France," said Élise. "Then *pour l'amour du ciel*—for heaven's sake, keep to the left!" Laughing, they all stood up, plates in hand, and headed toward the kitchen doors.

Course Nine—*Entremet*

Pronounced "aun-truh-may," this is a sweet dish.

....

J'adore la Fraise—I Love Strawberries
Serves 4-6

Ingredients
½ tablespoon butter
8 ounces strawberries, hulled and halved lengthwise
2 teaspoons cornstarch
3 eggs
1 cup milk
⅔ cup flour
¼ cup granulated sugar
1 ½ teaspoons vanilla
¼ teaspoon salt
Powdered sugar

Preparation
Preheat oven to 350°F. Grease a 2-quart baking or gratin dish with the butter. Toss strawberry halves with cornstarch until evenly coated, then arrange berries, cut side down, in bottom of dish and set aside.

In a blender, whirl eggs, milk, flour, granulated sugar, vanilla, and salt 15 seconds. Pour batter over strawberries.

Bake until puffed, golden brown, and set in the center, about 50 minutes. Dust with powdered sugar and serve warm.

Pairing Note
Enjoy this course with Crémant de Bourgogne, a sparkling rosé produced in the Champagne region of France.

....

Sis Boom Bah!

"Our behavior toward each other is the strangest, most unpredictable, and most unaccountable of all the phenomena with which we are obliged to live. In all of nature, there is nothing so threatening to humanity as humanity itself."

—**LEWIS THOMAS,** physician, etymologist, policy advisor, and author

For a moment, think of yourself as a business. In our personal lives, creativity and self-expression—everything we say and do—is the counterpart to marketing and sales in the business arena including public relations, brand recognition, and graphic identity.

Establishing and maintaining an excellent reputation is important. What are your answers to the following questions:

1. How do I present myself?
2. How does the world see me?
3. How do I want the world to see me?
4. If there's a difference between how the world sees me and how I want the world to see me, what action steps are required on my part to close the gap, to align the two perspectives?

And while your product or service may speak to a broad group of people, who—*specifically*—is your target audience? Trying to please everyone dilutes your efforts and frustrates your momentum because you can't please everyone.

Identify your target audience and do everything to ensure that they fall in love with the product or service you offer.

In his article "The Value of a Good Reputation" Alex Lickerman M.D. says, "Your reputation lives a very real existence apart from you."

He continues, "Our reputation represents the way others look at us and as such is at once critically important and utterly trivial. Utterly trivial because if we have a healthy self-esteem, we won't need others to think well of us (though many of course do struggle with this and often find their sense of value vulnerable to the opinions of others—especially their perception of the collective opinions of others).

"Critically important, however, because even those of us with resilient self-esteem live in a great social network and need a good reputation for practical purposes—friendship and income chief among them. It's hard to have friends if people think you're mean-spirited and hard to make a living in any capacity if people think you're lazy, unreliable, or dishonest."[5]

Collective Consciousness—
A Source for Individual Potential

Life is set in the framework of human relationships. John Hagelin, PhD, Quantum Physicist, and Educator is a forerunner in an exceedingly intricate, leading-edge area of science called unified field theory (UFT), which points to all of us being interconnected through the fabric of collective consciousness.

When we're mindful of our personal energy signature it has a positive influence on others. If we neglect to cultivate and maintain it, it can adversely affect others.

You've heard the saying "Never underestimate the power of one." It's true. Each of us has a sphere of influence. Whether we're a global citizen like the Dalai Lama or a local citizen, what we think, say, and do has far-reaching and lasting ramifications. Like putting a hand in wet cement, it leaves an impression long after we've left the scene. We exercise wisdom when we're mindful of our influence on others.

The interconnected wholeness of life—collective consciousness—can be likened to a bank of knowledge, understanding, history, and folklore—the source—that we can access. Each of us has a personal account with an inexhaustible balance. It's a wealth of infinite possibilities from which we can draw.

In my mind's eye, I picture people as individual stars orbiting the source—the constellation of collective consciousness. The information contained in this universe-size cache is an existing potential for each of us to tap into.

As with stars, some orbit closer to the source while others circle farther away. The ones traveling closer have the opportunity to listen deeply; they have the potential to gather wisdom from a well deeper than their own. It takes individual stars to create the breathtaking, star-studded tapestry of the nighttime sky—a collective effort—and so with each person.

Individually we have the opportunity to answer two unspoken questions:

1. How consciously shall I live?
2. How close to the source do I want my course to be?

The vast intelligence and wisdom that's available to us flow in an unbroken lineage from the birthing of the cosmos into you and me.

When we risk opening ourselves to a deep listening of this heritage—the source—we can create a compassion-filled world, one that recognizes and celebrates the differences in others be they religion, culture, socioeconomic status, sexual orientation, or political affiliation. *Omnes mundum facimus* is Latin for "We all make the world." A global village, our words and actions impact each other.

A profound example of this was eloquently displayed by one of Japan's greatest industrialists Konosuke Matsushita the founder of Panasonic when he said, "The untrapped mind is *open* enough to see many possibilities, *humble* enough to learn from anyone and anything, *forbearing* enough to *forgive* all, *perceptive* enough to see things as they really are, and reasonable enough to *judge* their true value."[6]

Imagine the positive global impact if every person made an effort to live these six values: openness, humility, forbearance, forgiveness, perception, and judgment. I believe this type of heart-based living—a life lived close to the source—would constructively influence every layer of society. The ripple effect would change the vibration of earth.

The camel driver in Paul Coelho's book *The Alchemist* observed that "all of our life stories and the history of the world were written by the same hand." There's that interconnection again. It's my belief that each of us has an undeniable responsibility to our self and the rest of the world to be our personal best on any given day. The ripple effect is far too reaching to do otherwise.

By sharing ourselves authentically with others, we afford them the opportunity to include us in their circle, or not. Pretending to be something we're not to fit in is exhausting, but when people accept us for who we are—the real deal—it's effortless to be our authentic selves.

Word of mouth is beyond doubt the best type of marketing there is. Virtually free, it's a matter of people telling others how much they like you. On the flip side of that coin is the familiar adage, "Good news travels fast. Bad news travels faster."

One way or another, we can count on the fact that word is going to circulate. That's why it's imperative both personally and professionally to conduct our lives in a manner that's positive, uplifting, constructive, and healing.

The Ripple Effect—Boomerang Style

Newton's Third Law of Motion states, "To every action, there is an equal and opposite reaction."[7] The same can be said for choices. For every choice there is a consequence. Be it positive or negative, there is always a consequence.

If we are, indeed, interconnected, everything we do—or fail to do— has a powerful ripple effect. Incredibly potent in that the consequences don't just extend outward but travel back again, boomerang-style. Some people refer to this as karma.

○ If I hurt you, I hurt myself and eventually harm my children and grandchildren.

○ If I lie to you, I lie to myself and in due course deceive my children and grandchildren.

○ If I steal from you, I steal from myself and ultimately take from my children, my grandchildren, and so on.

Likewise, when I do something that's positive, uplifting, constructive, and healing, the same boomerang-style (ripple) effect comes into play. Our thoughts and actions don't just affect us individually; they affect us collectively. The ramifications of what we think, say, and do aren't just local in nature; the impact is global.

You've heard the sayings, "What goes around comes around," and "You reap what you sow." On a surface level, that's one way of defining karma—often referred to as the law of return. *Karma* is a Sanskrit word that means "volitional action."

There are multiple schools of thought on this subject. I agree with the perspective that we're spiritual beings on a human journey; we're here on a temporary layover in the classroom called life for the specific purpose of learning lessons before continuing. Some people refer to these experiences as karma.

Enzo, the old soul and canine narrator of Garth Stein's book, *The Art of Racing in the Rain,* says, "I know that karma is a force in this universe and that people will receive karmic justice for their actions. I know that this justice will come when the universe deems it appropriate and it may not be in this lifetime but in the next, or the one after that. Their current consciousness may never feel the brunt of the karma they have incurred, though their souls absolutely will. I understand this concept."

The explanation of karma differs somewhat between cultural and spiritual traditions, but the general idea is the same. Through the law of karma—cause and effect—the result of every action creates present and future experiences, making each of us responsible for our life and the pain and joy it brings to those in our sphere of influence.

How would you react to this statement? "May you get exactly what you deserve." Depending on how you live your life, this could be a blessing or a curse.

I believe the karmic litmus test is to examine the motives that underlie our present actions—why we choose to take (active) or refrain from taking (passive) action. Despite how the past may account for many of the inequalities we see in life, the measure of a human being isn't the hand that's dealt them; it's how they play their hand. Because we're interconnected, our decisions affect everyone.

What's your ripple effect?

"How people treat you is their karma; how you react is yours."

—**WAYNE DYER,** self-help advocate, lecturer, and author

SECTION TEN

Product Launch

La Mandarine Bleue

Course Ten—*Savoureux*

Me, Myself, and I

Product Launch

"When talking to first-time entrepreneurs, I often ask them: 'How do you know that people want your product or service?' As you can expect, the answer is often that they don't yet, but will know once they launch. And they're right. That's why it's critical to launch as quickly as possible so you can get that feedback."

—**KATHRYN MINSHEW,** CEO and co-founder of
The Muse, a career-development platform

A study done by *Inc.* magazine and the National Business Incubator Association (NBIA) revealed that eighty percent of new businesses fail within the first five years.[1]

There's risk when launching a product, but that's part of the excitement!

According to Harvard Business School Professor Thomas Eisenmann, "Most startups are hamstrung from the start because they create the wrong product. A product launch is a guaranteed failure if you create the wrong product."[2]

Assumptions aren't facts; they're opportunities for research and testing. MarketingResearch.org expounds, "Strong assumptions often steer the new product development process; however, these assumptions may take you off course. A structured research process, rather than assumptions, will guide you toward a successful product launch."[3]

An effective strategy for launching a product is to create a website that attracts traffic and generates excitement and where you can gather potential customers by utilizing an email capture form. This will keep them updated and allow you to receive feedback from those potential customers. Customer response before launch is vital.

The *Wall Street Journal* calls Neil Patel "a top influencer on the web." *Forbes* says, "He is one of the top ten online marketers." *Entrepreneur Magazine* says, "He created one of the hundred most brilliant companies in the world."

Why do I share this information about Neil Patel with you? Because when he speaks, companies listen. When it comes to launching a product he says, "New products can be risky. Instead of spending years of your life and millions of dollars on a feature-rich product, create what can you with what you have. You can iterate features later, as you buy time, earn revenue, and respond to feedback.

"Apple is a great example of producing **minimum viable products**. The first iPad didn't have a camera, let alone the speed and visual **panache** of its more recently-released cousins. Launching sooner often trumps launching better."[4]

Practicing a product launch is important. James Hackett, the former CEO of Steelcase described how his company rehearsed product launch: "By building practice into our formal process, we make sure everyone is given the time and resources they need to do it and do it thoroughly. If the effort is worth our collective time and we are playing to win, then we need to practice to perform. Practice, in this case, meant training everyone from the line workers who had to adapt their production protocols to the sales force and order management people to the board members who would be asked about the product line once it went public."[5]

In his *Forbes* article "8 Elements of a Robust Product Launch Strategy" Neil Patel discusses pivoting. "Great companies know how to launch a product. But they also know how to pivot—to make a major directional change based on user feedback.

"Product launches are perfect pivotal moments. When your new product hits the market, you will immediately gain feedback on its success or lack thereof. Whether the response is positive or negative is inconsequential to this fact: The company must change.

"Regardless of the outcome, when you launch your product, you'll have an opportunity to change your company for the better."[6]

But What If I Fail?

Business or personal, chances are you're doing what you're passionate about. You're doing what you love. You're selling or promoting something you believe in. Your proposition is an extension of yourself.

How then do you not take rejection personally when it's your idea, your product, your service that's being turned down? Rejection is uncomfortable; it hurts. It can cause us to tip-toe around decisions for fear we might get turned down. It can cause us to agonize over perceived inadequacies.

In *The War of Art*, author Steven Pressfield says, "A professional distances herself from her instrument. The pro stands at one remove from her instrument—meaning her person, her body, her voice, her talent; the physical, mental, emotional, and psychological being she uses in her work. She does not identify with this instrument. It is simply what God gave her, what she has to work with. She assesses it coolly, impersonally, objectively."

The message here is to stop identifying with your work because it isn't you. It's something else—a tool, a resource, something of use. If it gets rejected, you scrap it or fix it, but you don't lose sleep over it. In separating yourself from your work, you're liberated.

In her *Huffington Post* article "11 Things I Wish I Knew When I Started My Business," writer, life strategist, and entrepreneur Stephanie St.Claire asks, "Does Madonna walk around the house in cone bras and come-f*k-me bustiers? She's too busy planning D-Day. Madonna does not identify with 'Madonna.' Madonna employs 'Madonna.'"

I love that perspective! Now if my work is rejected I'll look at it objectively to see how it can be improved. This viewpoint—what the Navajo call *"hozho"*—is similar to the Buddhist idea of seeking detachment. Attachment, particularly to outcomes, is the source of pain and suffering.

But in the event you're not in a zen frame of mind right now, here are the eleven things Stephanie St.Claire wishes she'd known when she started her business:

○ *Running the business is your first priority.* You'll spend fifteen percent of the time doing what you love and eighty-five percent of the time marketing, administrating, selling, strategizing your business, and answering a shitload of email.

○ *Ready to meet your soulmate? It's you.* Entrepreneurship is the most life changing relationship (like marriage or parenthood) that a person can have. You will be confronted overandoverandover with your fears, your insecurities, your crappy excuses, your limitations, your justifications, your shitty integrity, and your inefficient time management.

○ *Your trajectory for success will take as long as everyone else's, even though you're special and brilliant.* I heard the 'two-year rule' when I started by biz, but I was confident I could do it in six months. Jesus had other plans. See #4.

○ *Running out of money is a common part of the journey.* The good news is this is a rite of passage that will launch you into the League of Business Badassery in which, once you are out of the one hellhole, you will be unstoppable.

○ *Build a hybrid stream of income.* If having a steady stream of part-time income would be in service to your peace of mind, do it.

○ *Do the work.* The biggest challenge you will deal with in running a business is your own resistance. Period, end of story.

○ *Spend less time researching, more time doing.* Block out distractions (turn off the phone, social media, and email notifications) and take inspired action that feels tangible and measurable. Set a timer for twenty-five minutes and go to town on a task. Do not look up. Do not go to the bathroom. Do not cruise the fridge for cheese sticks. Get something done, despite the fact that at times you will feel like you are pissing into the wind. Piss into the wind four times a day, and you'll make a difference in your bottom line.

○ *Only say yes to clients/collaborative projects that are HELL YESes.* Scrutinize any joint project carefully and qualify the person you are doing the project with (even if they are your friend and have more page likes than you). Get everything in writing before you embark on the project, with a clear division of labor and deadline dates.

○ *You must devote time to become a brilliant marketer. Must.* I know you just want to spend all your days making hipster sarsaparilla-scented mustache wax, or needle pointing edgy throw pillows for Etsy, or writing your YA zombie novel, or life coaching women to stratospheric success, but if you don't spend time marketing you will not make money.

○ *Email will be your new best frenemy.* Your inbox will explode. You care about everyone, but you can't help everyone. Read: Not everyone is your customer. Your inbox will be a jumble of people who want to say thank you, people who want free stuff, and people who want your services. Your job is to quickly discern who's who and respond in the most appropriate way.

○ *Well, it's a hodge-podge.* Do not work your business seven days a week. From time to time, forget everything you know about the 'right way' to run a business and run it like a neighborhood lemonade stand. Do not price your offerings around your personal ability to pay for it—you are not your ideal customer.[7]

"Consumer habits are key to understanding how to launch a product."

—**CHARLES DUHIGG**, Pulitzer Prize-winning reporter at the *New York Times* and author

La Mandarine Bleue

"You have to check in every day and ask yourself what you want and what you're willing to give up. That's the way you cook with integrity every day."

—**JESSICA KOSLOW,** chef and restauranteur

The wrought-iron bistro tables and chairs for the dining patio arrived the same day as the pre-opening dress rehearsal was scheduled. With no time to deal with the furniture, Bill directed the delivery truck to follow him to his garage where they offloaded the oversized boxes for unpacking at a later date. Because the night's event was private, by invitation only, they didn't plan to use the outdoor seating.

"You're killing it," Amina said admiringly to Élise and Henri upon seeing them in their classic double-breasted chef's whites with the distinctive knot-button fronts. "Hey, I thought chefs wore tall white hats?" she questioned.

"Some chefs still wear the *toque blanche*, but mostly for formal appearances," Élise responded. "A bit more laid-back, we wear chef bandanas for practical purposes. They don't slip when we move fast, which is constantly, and they have built-in terry sweatbands. A must when working in a hot kitchen."

Amina noticed that Larry, Hannah, and Daniel also wore chef's bandanas, but instead of chef's whites, they had on bibbed white chef's aprons designed to stand up to the rigors of the kitchen. Unlike Élise and Henri's hound's-tooth chef pants, they wore solid black pants, and everyone in the kitchen wore strapped bistro clogs designed for slip resistance and comfort. Food industry professionals and everyone back of house know that working in a restaurant kitchen is a bit like being in the triage unit of a hospital; everything must run smoothly even in high-pressure situations. Only there is no blood—*hopefully.*

Last minute preparations were underway out front. Abbie, who'd accepted the position after speaking with her parents; Ethan; and the rest of the group—except Dwayne—were bring-it-on ready in blue and white chalk-stripe apron's over crisp white shirts. They too wore black pants and shoes. The women's sassy cobalt-blue bow ties were the perfect counterpart to the men's traditional ties, also cobalt-blue.

Peter's pinstripe waistcoat and black tie set him apart as the wine steward. The wine menu for this evening's event was ready with three offerings of each type:

VIN BLANC
○ Domaine Thomas Clos de la Crele 2014, Sauvignon Blanc, France—Sancerre
○ Chablis, Domaine Laroche "St. Martin" 2015, Chardonnay, France—Burgundy, Chablis
○ Pinot Auxerrois, Domaine Saint-Remy, Lieu-dit Val Saint-Gregoire 2015, Pinot Blanc, France—Alsace

VIN ROSÉ
○ Chateau Les Crostes 2015 Rosé Blend, France—Côtes de Provence
○ Domaine La Voute du verdus, Languedoc, 2014, Cinsault/Syrah
○ Chateau de La Clapiere, Côtes de Provence, Cru Classé, 2015, Grenache/Cinsault

VIN ROUGE
○ Domaine Laroche de la Chevalière 2014, Pinot Noir, France—Pay d'Oc

○ Château Croix-Mouton 2015, Red Bordeaux Blend, France—Bordeaux Supérieur
○ Chateau d'Or et de Gueules "Trassegum" 2013, Red Rhone Blend, France—Rhone, Costières de Nîmes

SPARKLING
○ Veuve Clicquot "Yellow Label—Brut" NV Champagne Blend, France—Champagne, Reims
○ Moët & Chandon "Ice Imperial" NV Champagne Blend, France—Champagne, Épernay
○ Louis Roederer "Cristal" Brut 2007, Champagne Blend, France—Champagne, Reims

CHAMPAGNE
○ Moët & Chandon "Impérial" NV Champagne Blend, France—Champagne
○ Perrier Jouet "Grand Brut" NV Champagne Blend, France—Champagne
○ Perrier-Jouët "Belle Epoque" 2006, Champagne Blend, France—Champagne

To preserve everyone's sanity, Sally and Zoe sent invitations with staggered arrival times. They explained that the event was a preview. "We're giving ourselves the opportunity to iron any wrinkles out of the fabric by using you as guinea pigs. We need your honest reactions to help us make sure we get things right. As our way of saying thank you, the evening is complementary. *On the house.*"

By the end of the first hour, forty guests had arrived and were in various stages of the dining experience; some were just beginning while others were ready to enjoy dessert.

From previous restaurant experience, Abbie and Ethan knew that communal platters are served from the left and removed from the right while artfully-plated individual meals and wine are served from the right and withdrawn from the left. They'd also mastered the art of "reading a table." Falling into a smooth rhythm—tuning into the cues offered by each other's body language without the need to say a single word—they were able to convey whether a diner was satisfied or needed further attention.

Like a bee flitting from blossom to blossom, Peter traveled from table to table, helping guests pair wines with their orders. The *oohs* and *aahs* were loud and plentiful. The comments included "Extraordinary," "My compliments to the chef," "Remarkable," "Delicious," "Oh my God!" "Splendid," and "Impressive."

After the last satisfied guest had left and the door was locked, the owners and staff sat down over a glass of wine to dissect the evening. Abbie, the youngest, had just turned twenty-one, so she was able to join them.

Bill said, "Family is the most important thing in life. Sometimes it's the one you're born into and sometimes it's the one you make for yourself. Let's raise our glasses to our family at *La Mandarine Bleue* and a job well done."

"*A bientôt*—cheers!"

Sheila said, "Our guests seemed to respond to us with enthusiasm."

Turning to Élise and Henri, Peter observed, "Everyone commented on how fantastic the food was."

Élise and Henri included Daniel and Hannah in the compliment. "We couldn't have done it without these two in the kitchen."

Looking at Abbie and Ethan, Sally said, "I heard many comments about how meticulous the service was." Then turning to Peter, she continued, "As one woman put it, your wine pairings were 'divine.'"

Amina observed, "We did what we set out to do. Our personal best. I think the reward was in meeting the challenge."

With the exception of Bill, they stripped tables, washed floors, loaded the dishwashers, and cleaned the kitchen and bathrooms. A huge *Hobbit* and *Lord of the Rings* fan, Daniel quoted J.R.R. Tolkien, "If more of us valued food and cheer and song above hoarded gold, it would be a merrier world."

While the rest focused on the tasks at hand, Bill packed up the evening's leftovers in to-go containers and drove to Rhodes Skate Park where a small contingent of homeless people—who for various reasons can't tolerate shelters—hang out under the bridge. They gratefully received his offerings.

The following morning, the *Idaho Statesman* ran an article complete with color photographs:

"*La Mandarine Bleue's* executive chef, Élise Fournier and pastry chef Henri Fournier, serve up traditional French cuisine with expertly paired wines in newly renovated space in Boise's 8th Street Restaurant Row. Clean lines and French accents define the casual yet stylish dining area.

"Committed to an authentic French kitchen, food, and wine, there's not a heat lamp or microwave to be found. The husband and wife chef team explained, "We don't freeze our food, so everything is fresh every day. It's all about quality and sourcing as local as we can. In keeping with the season, the menu will change every three months.

"Meticulous service in a warm and friendly atmosphere *La Mandarine Bleue* satisfies parties of every size; their fresh-forward, expertly prepared lunch and dinner menus include communal dishes as well as individual choices.

"By-the-glass, half bottle, and bottle selections on the all-French wine list are not inexpensive, but look close and there are a couple bargains to be had.

"They also offer fair-weather patio seating and separate, second-floor space for private parties, corporate meetings, conferences, and seminars.

"Insider tip: Save room for dessert! We had a sampling of each; you can't go wrong.

"Must order: *Pore à la Dijonnaise*—sautéed pork tenderloin medallions with an orange compare sauce.

"Grand Opening: Mother's Day—make your reservations now."

Course Ten—*Savoureux*

Pronounced "savoury," this course is for guests who don't want sweets at the end of a meal.

. . . .

Pouding au Pain de Poireaux et Champignons—
Leek and Mushroom Bread Pudding
Serves 8–10

Ingredients
> 6 cups (½-inch-diced) bread cubes from a rustic country
>   loaf, crusts removed
> 2 tablespoons good olive oil
> 1 tablespoon unsalted butter
> 2 ounces pancetta, small-diced
> 4 cups sliced leeks, white and light green parts (4 leeks)
> 1 ½ pounds cremini mushrooms, stems trimmed and
>   ¼-inch-sliced
> 1 tablespoon chopped, fresh tarragon leaves
> ¼ cup medium or dry sherry
> Kosher salt and freshly ground black pepper
> ⅓ cup minced, fresh flat-leaf parsley
> 4 extra-large eggs
> 1 ½ cups heavy cream

1 cup chicken stock, preferably homemade

1 ½ cups grated gruyere cheese (6 ounces), divided

Preparation

Preheat the oven to 350°F. Spread the bread cubes on a sheet pan and bake for 15 to 20 minutes until lightly browned. Set aside.

Meanwhile, heat the oil and butter in a large (12-inch) sauté pan over medium heat. Add the pancetta and cook for 5 minutes until starting to brown. Stir in the leeks, and cook over medium heat for 8 to 10 minutes until the leeks are tender. Stir in the mushrooms, tarragon, sherry, 1 tablespoon salt, and 1 ½ teaspoons pepper and cook for 10 to 12 minutes until most of the liquid evaporates, stirring occasionally. Off the heat, stir in the parsley.

In a large mixing bowl, whisk together the eggs, cream, chicken stock and 1 cup of the gruyere. Add the bread cubes and mushroom mixture, stirring well to combine. Set aside at room temperature for 30 minutes to allow the bread to absorb the liquid. Stir well and pour into a 2 ½-to-3-quart gratin dish (13 x 9 x 2 inches). Sprinkle with the remaining 1/2 cup gruyere and bake for 45 to 50 minutes until the top is browned and the custard is set. Serve hot.

Pairing Note

Enjoy the course with Jasnières, a white wine from the Loire Valley region of France.

Me, Myself, and I

"To me, self-esteem is not self-love. It is self-acknowledgment, as in recognizing and accepting who you are."

—**AMITY GAIGE**, novelist

For a moment, think of yourself as a business. In our personal lives, self-confidence in what we stand for—our purpose, mission, path, passion, and philosophy—is the counterpart of a product launch in the business world.

This section of the book isn't about the shameless art of self-adulation—crowing about our accomplishments, tooting our own horn, or self-applause. It's not about conceit, egotism, or self-admiration.

Remember the guy in Greek mythology—Narcissus— who gazed endlessly at his reflection in a pool? So endlessly that "he slowly pined away and was transformed by the nymphs into a narcissus flower."[8]

Narcissus is where we get the term "narcissist." The dictionary defines "narcissism" as an "inordinate fascination with oneself; excessive self-love; vanity."[9]

There's a tremendous difference between self-adulation (a cocky braggart) and self-confidence. The people in our sphere of influence—our "tribe"—appreciate our ideas and vision because they understand it's not about us; it's about how they fit in.

In *Note to Self: A Seven-Step Path to Gratitude and Growth* I share that personal power and self-definition work hand in hand with social wellness—our ability to relate to the people around us in a pleasant, honest, and authentic manner. It includes using excellent verbal and nonverbal communication skills, respecting ourselves and others, and participating in a supportive structure of encouragement that includes friends and family.

Every person wants to be validated—heard, respected, and valued—instead of tolerated or rejected. Validation gives us a sense of belonging, a sense that we're part of something bigger than we are.

At the offices or in our homes, in business or our personal lives, validation is a two-way street:

○ We must listen if we want to be heard.
○ We must esteem others if we want to be respected.
○ We must appreciate others if we want to be valued.
○ We must accept—not merely tolerate—others if we want to be included.

People who experience social wellness (a vital component of self-confidence) value living in harmony, in unity. They actively reach out to cultivate and nurture relationships based on mutual commitment, trust, and respect. This fosters a willingness to share thoughts and feelings. One of the hallmarks of social wellness is being inclusive, not exclusive, with our friendship.

In taking an active role, we come to understand and value that self-confidence enhances our ease when being outgoing and building a friendly rapport; it makes it easier to be open with and approachable by others while maintaining healthy boundaries.

We all need relationships. The healthier our relationships, the better we feel toward other individuals and the global community as a whole.

Unity, though concerned with the larger group—the whole—is birthed by individuals—you and me. I see unity as having two orientations:

- *Vertically*—our connection to that which is bigger than ourselves (source energy, divinity)
- *Horizontally*—our connection with the people around us

The intersection of these two lines is the seat of compassion—the key ingredient for unity at its best.

Identification with a group is vital to how we define ourselves. The worth of any group lies in the behavior of its individual members. Every group has many people who are positive contributors. And of course, every group has people who are otherwise.

Connecting with like-minded people helps to make us aware of our inherent unity. When we're warmly included—validated—it nurtures a warm sense of belonging, a sense that we're part of something bigger than ourselves.

One of my clients, an aspiring writer, shared, "I wish I weren't so shallow, but sadly, honestly, I am. I wait for validation. I wait for recognition. I wait to be invited—by him, by her, by them, by the publishing world. While I wait, I sharpen the tools of my craft, and I dream."

Being our authentic self within a group is vital. Frank Lloyd Wright, the father of organic architecture, said, "The reality of a building is the space within. And what you put into that space will affect how you live in it and what you become. Don't clutter the place with stuff that does not enable it."

His point is that it's the details that express the whole. This is equally true of our personal ecology—inner landscape—that brings us back to the beginning. Unity, though concerned with the larger group, is birthed by individuals when we're at our compassion-filled, authentic best.

It's wonderful being with other people and sharing undivided attention. However, it becomes lackluster when their attention is divided. For example, have you ever been with someone whose smartphone absorbed their attention?

In his TED talk, psychologist Daniel Goleman tells us there's a newly coined word in the English language for the moment when the person we're with whips out their smartphone and all of a sudden we don't exist. The word is *"pizzled,"*—a combination of puzzled and pissed off.[10]

Goleman goes on to say, "It's our empathy, our tuning in with others, which separates us from Machiavellians and sociopaths." Being present when we're with others is a blue-ribbon choice. Being present when we're by ourselves is also a winning choice.

Let's drill a little deeper and take a closer look at empathy and its cousins pity, sympathy, and compassion:

Pity is a thought that usually results from an encounter with an unfortunate or injured person, animal, or situation. It usually ends here—a mental acknowledgment that isn't followed by action steps.

Sympathy is a feeling of concern for another, the desire to see them better off or happier. It can include being personally affected emotionally by an encounter.

Empathy is more than the recognition of another's suffering. Often characterized as the ability to put oneself into another's shoes, it's a combination of thinking and feeling—a deep emotional resonance that can spark a desire to alleviate another's suffering. It's responding to the needs of others *based on how we feel*.

Compassion is a profound and positive emotion prompted by the pain of others. More vigorous than empathy, the feeling commonly gives rise to actions that work toward alleviating another person's suffering. It's responding to the needs of others *regardless of how we feel*.

Science tells us that when we experience sustained positive emotions like compassion, care, forgiveness, gratitude, and patience, our body produces dehydroepiandrosterone (DHEA), which is secreted by the adrenal glands. DHEA is known as the vitality hormone; it accelerates renewal and improves our health.

When we experience sustained negative emotions such as anger, bitterness, worry, or fear, our bodies produce cortisol, which contributes to sub-optimal performance, accelerates aging, and is degenerative to health. But one of these emotions—fear—can be good for us.

Fear Provides Us with the Opportunity to Slay Dragons

Fear is in the heart of the beholder. One woman's fear may be another woman's strength. It's been said that the best way to eliminate an enemy is to make him your friend. It's the same with fear; we can cultivate fear as a friend.

There are many types of fear: social, emotional, and physical among them. Regardless of the type, fear is not only a great survival tool, it shows us what's important and what matters to us.

Do you experience stage fright just before delivering a presentation or get tongue-tied and flustered when meeting new people? Do you become anxiety-ridden at the dentist's office or feel panicky when stepping into a small space or onto an airplane?

Fear can be debilitating; it can cause us to freeze in our tracks (emotionally or otherwise), cutting us off at the knees.

Fear can be a leverage point (emotionally or otherwise), helping us get from Point A to Point B.

Fear is an excellent guide to opportunity. It dares us to rise to the challenge, to step into courage and confront that which makes us afraid. It can be the catalyst that motivates us to action: perhaps expressing our opinion in a group setting despite the fear of being ostracized or ending a relationship that's bankrupting our heart.

The world without fear would be dangerous. Like any good friend, fear—and its cousin adrenaline—lets us know when to freeze, fight, or flee—*run like the dickens!* They call us to action. Fear provides the energy and motivation to do what needs to be done.

Each person's situation is different. One person may need to practice their presentation so they know it inside out. Another may need to say "no"—and stick with it—regardless of the reception it receives.

One of my clients said, "Laurie, how can you possibly relate to what I'm going through? You have a perfect life—you don't have anything to be afraid of." Let me be the first to say that her perception of me isn't accurate. But as I shared with her, I've made it a practice to set my fears down so I can stand on them like a footstool and step up into joy.

Fear lets us know we're alive. Without fear life would be flat; there'd be no effervescence. Fear provides us with the opportunity to slay dragons. Once defeated, we get the thrill of fist-punching the air and shouting *Woohoo!* as we sashay on to the next conquest.

Don't Outsource Your Life—Live It Yourself

If you do an internet search, you'll quickly learn that from laundry to dating, you can outsource just about everything.

The Sydney Morning Herald featured an article titled "Spend Time, Not Money and Don't Outsource Your Life" in which journalist Karen Hardy interviewed a woman who spends $6,500 per week (yes, you read that correctly) outsourcing domestic tasks, childcare, and part of her workload.

This woman has a live-in nanny, three cleaners, an executive assistant, and a researcher. Why? She said, "I simply could not do it all, maintain a practice and be nearly human."

She went on to say that, "Outsourcing is the only way I can run my legal practice, get enough sleep and exercise, and make quality time for my family." But she admits that with all this, it (quality time) boils down to two hours per day—the *quality* time with her husband and children.

You see, spending time with them isn't billable. She can't make money if she's chauffeuring them to events, helping them with homework, reading a book or watching a movie with them, teaching them to bake cookies, or walking the dog. There's no income involved if she enjoys a glass of wine by the fire in the evening with her husband.

Hardy concluded that "Perhaps if Ms. Nolan stopped outsourcing she'd find more than two hours a day to spend with her husband and children." She concluded the article saying she would never want to be that "successful."[11]

Yes, there are services out there that let men outsource their online dating tasks to paid wingmen. CNN ran a piece titled "Don't Outsource Your Dating Life." It starts, "Critics haven't been kind to Personal Dating Assistants, a new service that allows men to up their online dating game by outsourcing tasks to paid, clandestine wingmen who pimp profiles, locate prospects, and ghostwrite correspondences. GQ calls it 'creepy.' CNET says customers eventually will have to admit they are big fakes. And over at *Jezebel*, dudes who take advantage of the deception are called 'human trash.'"[12]

The point of sharing these stories with you is to highlight the fact that this is *your* life—the pleasant aspects, the not so pleasant aspects, and everything in between. *You're* the quality factor in your life. You. Personally. To delegate your life is to not live it. Time is precious, so sharing ourselves with others gifts them with two of the most valuable commodities we have: our time and ourselves.

What does your authentic self look like? Not the exterior package you reside in but your essence. When you examine your self-portrait, what does it reveal about you—your impact on the earth and its inhabitants?

1. Are you a creator or a destroyer?
2. Are you responsible or irresponsible?
3. Does your life reveal what inspires you?
4. Do you transcend the superficial?
5. Does your self-portrait reflect gratitude?

If, upon close examination, you don't care for what you see, acknowledge it, change it, and move forward. You're the artist; select different colors. You're the author; write a different story. You're the composer; choose different notes. Redefine yourself. No—*amaze* yourself!

"Self-doubt is real. Everyone has it. Having confidence and losing confidence is real, too, and everyone has been in that position."

—VENUS WILLIAMS, professional tennis player

SECTION ELEVEN

Operations and Organization

La Mandarine Bleue

Course Eleven—*Fromage*

No Man Is an Island

Operations and Organization

"I think leadership is service and there is power in that giving: to help people, to inspire and motivate them to reach their fullest potential."

—**DENISE MORRISON,** President and CEO of
Campbell Soup Company

In her article "'Everyone is Replaceable' and Other Business Lies," Liz Ryan writes, "'Everyone is replaceable' is a lie, thankfully. If we were truly hiring people who could be replaced at any moment, we'd be doing a terrible disservice to our customers and shareholders. Yet we hear the expression all the time: 'Everyone is replaceable.' Really? What an awful thing to say, or to believe!"[1]

Companies are comprised of individuals—people. People are *not* expendable.

The Human Workplace (a publishing firm, think tank, coaching and consulting business in Boulder, Colorado) observes that "the energy blocks we see most often [in business] have to do with fear and trust. Energy gets dammed up in an organization, and people get frustrated when there's a big problem that no one is talking about; it's the elephant in the room.

"The elephant could be anything. It might be slipping market share or the fact that no one believes the upcoming product release is really what customers need.

"No one wants to name the elephant, but the energy field reflects the energy blockage nonetheless. Eventually, something erupts, and everyone looks around for someone to blame.

"We don't have to run our organizations that way. We can talk about fear and trust every day because fear and trust are business topics as surely as product returns and markdowns are.

"We can talk about feeling anxious and not being sure what to do next. It takes a real leader to be that honest with his or her team. People will follow a truth-telling leader to the ends of the earth. Can you be that strong as a leader?"[2]

> "Leadership is a potent combination of strategy and character. But if you must be without one, be without the strategy."
>
> —NORMAN SCHWARZKOPF, United States Army general

It's easy to identify what leadership isn't, but it's harder to find a consensus on what it is. After dozens of personal interviews and reading countless books and articles on leadership, the following is a list of twenty-six qualities that exceptional leaders have in common. The ABCs of leadership:

Aware—well informed
Benevolent—good intentions
Curious—eager to learn
Decisive—make decisions quickly and efficiently
Endurance—ability to withstand difficulties; resilient
Forward-looking—favors innovation and development
Grateful—an "attitude of gratitude"
Honorable—honest, moral, ethical, and principled
Inspiring—has the effect of uplifting someone
Just—behaves according to what is morally right and fair
Keen—sharp-minded
Life-long learner—actively pursues knowledge
Moxie—determination or nerve
Nimble—able to change direction quickly

Open—transparent and accountable
Perceptive—has or shows sensitive insight
Quality—focuses on quality over quantity
Respectful—shows deference and respect
Stable—models constancy and consistency
Thought leader—introduces new ways of thinking
United—joins others for a common purpose
Valiant—possesses courage and determination
Wise—has experience, knowledge, and good judgment
eXemplary—serves as a desirable model; representing the best of its kind
Young—at heart; a lively, positive attitude
Zealous—ardent, active, and devoted

Everyone can lead with excellence. Leadership isn't about titles or roles. At its heart, it's about influence—for better or worse.

"Never underestimate the influence you have on others."

—**LAURIE BUCHANAN,** holistic health practitioner, transformational life coach, and author

For better or worse, every choice we make influences our life and the people in our sphere of influence—our family, friends, colleagues, communities, even the environment. Mindful leadership is about being open to our wisdom so we can influence for better more often and for worse less often.

People who influence for better are leaders because they make a difference, and more importantly, because they inspire those around them to want to make a difference. Can you remember the actions or words of a person who's had a strong positive impact on you, someone who inspired you?

My fifth-grade teacher, Mrs. Kline, was this individual in my life. Her determined but gentle understanding changed the trajectory of my life. Having caught me several times reading on the sneak, she knew I love to read. She gave me the gift of the book *The Swiss Family Robinson* and asked me to use it to help classmates who were struggling with reading. She planted a seed—the desire to help others—in me that grew, blossomed, and still thrives.

Finding the Space to Lead: A Practical Guide to Mindful Leadership was authored by Janice Marturano, former vice president at General Mills, and founder and executive director of the Institute for Mindful Leadership. In it, she says, "In the decade since I began developing and teaching the mindful leadership curricula of the Institute for Mindful Leadership, I have seen that the best leaders are those with bright minds and warm hearts. They are people who want to make a difference."

Mindfulness is simple, but it's not easy. Jon Kabat-Zinn well-known author and founder of the Stress Reduction Clinic at the University of Massachusetts tells us that "mindfulness means paying attention in a particular way: on purpose, in the present moment, and non-judgmentally."[3]

Mindfulness is the open-hearted energy of being aware in the present moment. It's the daily cultivation—practice—of touching life deeply. To be mindful is to be present with, and sensitive to, our surroundings, the people we're with, and the things we're doing, whether we're raking leaves, tying our shoes, or preparing a meal.

It's my perspective that mindfulness is more than paying attention; it's paying intention. Paying attention engages the mind. Paying intention also engages the will.

Givers, Takers, and Matchers

Cubicle farms, plush offices, or a combination thereof, offices contain people with a variety of temperaments. In a TED talk, organizational psychologist Adam Grant says, "There are three types of personalities in the workplace: givers, takers, and matchers.

"*Takers* are self-serving in their interactions. It's all about 'what can you do for me?'

"*Givers* approach most interactions by asking 'What can I do for you?'"

After surveying over 30,000 people—across industries and cultures around the globe—Grant discovered that most people are in the middle of giving and taking; they're a third style called matching.

"*Matchers* try to keep an even balance of give and take, 'I'll do something for you if you do something for me.' And while that's a safe way to live life, it's not the most useful and productive way to live it."

After studying dozens of organizations and thousands of people, Grant asked engineers to measure their productivity. He also reviewed medical students' grades and sales people's revenue. He unexpectedly discovered that the worst performers in each of these jobs were the givers.

- The least productive engineers were the ones who did more favors than they got back.
- The lowest grades in medical school belong to students who agree most strongly with statements like 'I love helping others.'
- The lowest sales revenue was accrued by the most generous sales people.

Grant said he reached out to a sales person who had a high giver score and asked, "What's the cost of generosity in sales?" The person responded, "I just care so deeply about my customers that I would never sell them one of our crappy products."

It turns out there's a twist.

Givers often sacrifice themselves, but they make their organizations better. The quantity of evidence from measurable metrics show that organizations with giving behavior have lower operating expenses, high employee retention, customer satisfaction, and profits.

Givers spend significant time trying to help other people and improve the team and then, unfortunately, suffer for it.

What does it take to build cultures where givers get to succeed?

If givers are the worst performers, who are the best performers?

Grant says, "The good news is, it's not the takers. Takers tend to rise quickly, but also fall quickly in most jobs. And they fall at the hands of matchers.

"Matchers believe in an eye for an eye—a just world. So when they meet a taker, they feel it's their mission in life to punish the hell out of that person. And that way justice gets served.

"Most people are matchers. That means if you're a taker it tends to catch up with you eventually. What goes around will come around. So the logical conclusion is, it must be the matchers who are the best performers. But they're not."

In every job in every organization Adam Grant studied, the best results belonged to the givers—again. Givers go to both extremes. They make up the majority of the people who bring in the lowest revenue but also the highest revenue. He said, "Givers are over-represented at the bottom and at the top of every success metric that can be tracked."

How do we create cultures where givers excel? Adam Grant suggests three ways.

1. *Protect givers from burnout.* It's critical to recognize that givers are your most valuable people, but if they're not careful they burn out. So you have to protect the givers in your midst.

2. *Encourage help-seeking.* Successful givers recognize that it's ok to be a receiver too. If you run an organization, you can make it easier for people to ask for help.

In their study of hospitals, Grant and his colleagues found that on certain floors, nurses did a lot of help-seeking. But on other floors, hardly any. They observed, "The factors that stood out on the floors where help-seeking was common—where it was the norm—was there was just one nurse whose sole job it was to help other nurses on the unit. And when that role was available, nurses said 'Oh, it's not embarrassing, it's not vulnerable to ask for help. It's encouraged.'"

To build a culture of successful givers, Adam says, "The most important thing is to be thoughtful about who you let onto your team."

3. *Get the right people on the bus.* The negative impact of a taker on culture is more than double the positive impact of a giver. Effective hiring, screening, and team-building isn't about bringing in the givers; it's about weeding out the takers.

"If you can do that well, you'll be left with givers and matchers. The givers will be generous because they don't have to worry about the consequences. And the beauty of the matchers is that they follow the norm."

So how do we catch takers before it's too late?

Grant says, "We're pretty bad at figuring out who's a taker; especially on first impressions. And there's a personality trait that throws us off. It's called agreeableness. One of the major dimensions of personality across cultures.

"*Agreeable* people are warm and friendly; they're nice, they're polite.

"*Disagreeable* people do less of it (try to please other people). They're more critical, skeptical, and challenging."

Grant elaborates, "I had assumed that agreeable people were givers and disagreeable people were takers. But then I gathered the data, and I was stunned to find no correlation between those traits because it turns out that agreeableness and disagreeableness is an outer veneer. How pleasant [or not] it is to interact with you?

"Whereas giving and taking are inner motives. They're your values, your intentions toward others."

Grant says there are two other combinations we tend to forget about.

"There are *disagreeable givers* in our organizations—people who are gruff and tough on the surface but underneath have other's best interests at heart. Disagreeable givers are the most undervalued people in our organizations because they're the ones who give the critical feedback that no one wants to hear, but everyone needs to hear.

"We need to do a much better job valuing these people and not writing them off by thinking, 'Kind of prickly, must be a selfish taker.'

"The other combination we forget about is the deadly one—the *agreeable taker;* also known as the faker. This is the person who's nice to your face and will stab you in the back. My favorite way to catch these people in the interview process is to ask the question, 'Can you give me the names of four people whose careers you have fundamentally improved?'

"The takers will give you four names and they will all be more influential than them because takers are great at kissing up and then kicking down.

"Givers are more likely to name people who are below them in a hierarchy; who don't have as much power; who can do them no good.

And let's face it, we all know we can learn a lot about a person's character by watching how they treat a restaurant server or their Uber driver.

"If we can weed takers out of organizations; if we can make it safe to ask for help; if we can protect givers from burnout, and make it ok for them to be ambitious in pursuing their goals as well as trying to help other people, we can actually change the way that people define success.

"Instead of saying it's all about winning a competition, people will realize success is more about contribution."

Grant says, "I believe that the most meaningful way to succeed is to help other people succeed. If we can spread that belief, we can turn paranoia upside down. There's a name for that. It's called 'pronoia'—the delusional belief that other people are plotting your well-being; they're going around behind your back and saying exceptionally glowing things about you.

"The great thing about a culture of givers is that it's not a delusion, it's reality. I want to live in a world where givers succeed, and I hope you will help me create that world."[4]

If you're reading this book, you're probably like me; you want to be an active participant in creating a world where givers succeed.

"My father said there were two kinds of people in the world: givers and takers. The takers may eat better, but the givers sleep better."

—MARLO THOMAS, actress, producer, social activist, and author

La Mandarine Bleue

"I came to all the realizations about sustainability and bio-diversity because I fell in love with the way food tastes. And because I was looking for that taste I feel at the doorsteps of the organic, local, sustainable farmers, dairy people, and fisherman."

—**ALICE WATERS,** chef, restauranteur, activist, and author

The decision to have *La Mandarine Bleue's* grand opening on Mother's Day turned out to be brilliant!

Once the promotions appeared on their website, Facebook page, other social media platforms, in the *Idaho Statesman*, the *Idaho Press-Tribune*, and the *Boise Weekly*, the phone rang off the hook. Reservations were at capacity for brunch seating between 10:00 a.m. and 2:00 p.m. and dinner seating from 6:00 p.m. to 10:00 p.m. They'd voted unanimously to use patio seating for overflow—people who hadn't made reservations and were willing to risk availability. The investment in patio seating paid for itself their first day in business. Like a magnet, the opening day promo drew customers from Boise and the surrounding area.

"Let *La Mandarine Bleue* help you make Mother's Day memorable with delicious **prix-fixe** menus for brunch and dinner to celebrate the ladies you love.

BRUNCH INCLUDES:

○ *Quiche aux fines herbes aux tomates Heirloom*—herbed quiche with Heirloom tomatoes

○ *Gâteau au fromage aux framboises farcies pain grillé Français*—raspberry cheesecake stuffed French toast

○ *Sunshine crêpes avec fraises et zeste d'Orange*—sunshine crepes with strawberries and orange zest

○ Champagne

DINNER INCLUDES:

○ *La Bisque de Homard Safranee*—saffron lobster bisque

○ *Panais crémeuse et salade de pommes*—creamy parsnip and apple salad

○ *Filet Mignon avec Sauce truffée*—filet mignon with truffle sauce

○ *Mousse au chocolat blanc aux framboises*—white chocolate mousse with raspberries

○ Champagne"

Two years later, the wrought-iron bistro tables and chairs on the front patio of *La Mandarine Bleue* were still welcoming and cheerful. Set at jaunty angles, the cobalt umbrellas matched the logo and stripes on the awning, bringing to mind the pavement cafés in Paris. A **Gallic** ritual, many Parisians gather at outdoor *cafés* to start their day with a strong black coffee in the morning, *pastis*—an anise-flavored spirit—at lunchtime, and wine in the evening.

Teamwork and open communication are the oil that greases the wheels of the successful collaboration at *La Mandarine Bleue*. Each person has a job to do and does their personal best each day:

Sally and Zoe continued to focus on advertising, marketing, and public relations. Their ongoing efforts paid off—big time!

With eyes for three months into the future, Larry cheerfully continued researching potential recipes for the next season's menu freeing Élise and Henri to focus on the season and tasks at hand: cooking, baking, overseeing the kitchen staff, their prep work, and conducting the final examination of food prior to it being sent out to guests.

Once menus were approved, Peter researched wines to pair with them and set up private tastings with their local distributor who enjoys being part of their after-hours sampling events. As Peter prepared for a new challenge, they actively sought a *sommelier.*

Sheila ensured that the connection between kitchen and dining room ran smoothly.

Abbie, in the throes of her graduation year, only worked weekends. So, they hired another young woman—Isabella, quickly shortened to "Bella"—to pick up Abbie's hours.

When Ethan was promoted to *Maître d'*, they hired Michael to take over his previous responsibilities. Ethan began online courses for a hospitality degree in hotel and restaurant management.

With a large-scale art installation on the horizon, Amina and Yousef continued to step in—schedules permitting—to help whenever needed.

Bill continued to oversee the day-to-day finances and business affairs, but they hired an outside financial advisor, Heath, to manage their investments. A firm believer in good karma, each evening after the restaurant closed, Bill continued the practice of packing leftovers in to-go containers and driving to Rhodes Skate Park. Without fail, his offerings were received with gratitude.

Who could have known that Hannah would have such a way with pastries? She became pastry sous chef to Henri—doing the dessert prep work and keeping track of inventory. She was charged with the task of researching new recipes and suggested testing them at the Boise Capitol City Public Market on Saturdays. The desserts sold out quickly, and each sale included a promotional piece with a discount coupon for take-out baked goods from *La Mandarine Bleue.*

Henri's pastries were so popular they installed a bakery display case. And though the restaurant doesn't serve until lunchtime on weekdays, it's open for baked-fresh-this-morning takeaway pastry and coffee. While viewing the tempting variety, one woman said, "I gained a pound just looking!"

Daniel became sous chef to Élise. Jacob was hired as a part-time line cook to help during the busiest hours; he then started working at the restaurant full time.

Due to its popularity, the second-floor space for private parties, corporate meetings, conferences, and seminars started being used on a regular basis. It got so busy, they installed a commercial dumbwaiter (an electric lift) to carry food between the kitchen and the upstairs dining area.

The newest members of *La Mandarine Bleue's* family, Olivia and Joseph, were responsible for the upstairs guests. They sent orders to the kitchen from the serving station computer and received them via the lift.

Élise and Henri bought a loft in downtown Boise that put them within walking and bicycle distance to the greenbelt, the Boise River, all the parks, and everything downtown. Having learned the etymology of Boise on the internet, Henri is fond of sharing it: "In the 1820s, French-Canadian fur trappers set trap lines in the vicinity. Set in a high-desert area, the tree-lined valley of the Boise River became a distinct landmark, an oasis dominated by cottonwood trees. They called this '*La rivière boisée*,' which means 'the wooded river.'"[5]

Having bought into the business, Élise and Henri hosted their first meeting as owners at their loft. Dwayne, out on a book tour, was brought up to speed by Larry during one of their nightly phone conversations. Larry described the home's decor as "European elegance meets rustic country and old-world character," and explained that "the graceful and inviting style strikes the perfect balance of beauty and comfort."

Continuing he said, "The French-inspired kitchen is to die for! The hexagonal travertine floor tiles harmonize beautifully with the soft-hued yellow walls, vivid red accents, and reclaimed and distressed wood cabinets."

The group gathered in the cozy living room with a symmetrical arrangement of chairs around a large, low-set, distressed table. Striking in appearance, the dramatic chocolate-brown draperies elegantly framed the fireplace.

"You guys are guinea pigs," Élise said smiling. "We're testing recipes on you. In the meantime, please enjoy these *hors d'oeuvres—rillettes de canard*—duck roulette, with gherkins and toasts." And with that, Élise turned on her heel and returned to the kitchen to work with Henri.

Gazing around with interest, everyone was enjoying their first visit to Élise and Henri's loft. They all laughed when Sheila noted, "It's not surprising that the beautiful soft colors they've chosen to decorate with have food names: oyster, custard, pear, and chocolate."

Henri came to collect their empty plates. "I hope you saved room," he said rubbing his hands together. "We're serving family style, so please help yourselves." Nodding his head, he directed their gaze to the sideboard. "There are more dishes, flatware, and glasses over there. And please help yourselves to the wine."

Moments later, Élise and Henri reentered and offloaded two large serving trays onto the center table. The smell was heavenly. Pointing to each, Élise described them. "This is *salade de pommel locales*—local orchard apple salad with blue cheese mousse, arugula, reduced apple cider, and toasted walnuts. And this," she continued pointing to a different dish, "is *poulet sauté avec sauce à la crème estragon et carottes*—sautéed chicken with tarragon cream sauce and carrots."

Henri picked up where Élise left off. "And for dessert, we'll enjoy *biscuits au chocolat avec purée d'yuzu au gingembre, nougatine châtaigne et des glaces maison citrouille*—chocolate biscuits with yuzu ginger puree, chestnut nougatine, and homemade pumpkin ice cream."

By the time the quarterly business meeting wrapped up, they were stuffed. Everyone waddled out into the crisp air of the beautiful, early fall evening, happy they'd come on foot because they needed to burn calories by walking home.

Course Eleven—*Fromage*

Pronounced "fro-maaj," this course is the varietal cheese board.

Plateau de Fromages Français Classique—
Classic French Cheese Platter
Serve a wide range of block cheese, planning on approximately 2 ounces per person; adjust the amount according to other accompaniments you plan to serve.

Ingredients
   Etorki (bold)
   Saint Albray (rich)
   Roquefort (classic)
   Goat cheese (tangy)
   Brie (buttery)

Remove cheese from the refrigerator about an hour before serving. Present it on a flat surface—a board, slate, or a lovely tile will do. Provide each cheese with its own knife.

Serve with plain baguettes or plain crackers.

Cook's Note

Additional accompaniments might include crunchy nuts, strawberries, sweet pears, or pickled onions to create a savory contrast to the smooth cheeses.

Pairing Note

Enjoy this course with champagne, a sparkling white wine produced in the Champagne region of France.

....

No Man is an Island

"We are so much more than the sum of our parts. We are added, subtracted, multiplied, divided, in infinite variations. We are created again with every thought, experience, memory, and emotion. That equation takes more than a mind to understand; it takes heart and soul—synergy."

—**SHALA KERRIGAN,** craft goddess at Don't Eat the Paste

For a moment, think of yourself as a business. In our personal lives, synergy—interaction, teamwork, communication, and relationship management—is the counterpart of operations and organizations in the business arena.

Stakeholders in the business world—investors, customers, and clients—are equivalent to friends and family in our personal lives. Whether business or personal, trust, good communication, and healthy boundaries are vital ingredients in thriving relationships, in keeping the people in our sphere of influence engaged.

One of the principal reasons that relationships dissolve is *indifference.* Sending the message—actively or passively—that we don't care. On the other hand, enthusiasm—commitment, willingness, and involvement—actively demonstrates interest.

In the business world, there are three levels of customer service:

○ Baseline
○ Good
○ Exceptional

Have you ever wondered what makes your best friend your best friend? Or why you're a best friend to someone else? It's the *exceptional* factor. It's a result of knowing someone well—well enough to anticipate, to be proactive.

We give our repeat business to stores, brands, and restaurants because they deliver. It's the same with the people in our inner circle; they follow through. Our best friends retain that status because we can count on them. Likewise, they can rely on us. They give us their active attention, not passive intention. It's always disappointing to be on the receiving end of, "but I *intended* to," "I had good *intentions*," or "my *intentions* were in the right place." Our best friends are *attentive*, not *intentive*.

Scott Adams, the creator of the Dilbert comic strip, made a brilliant observation in his book *How to Fail at Almost Everything and Still Win Big: Kind of the Story of My Life* that's applicable in both our business and personal lives. He says, "The market rewards execution, not ideas."

Two Ears, One Mouth

In the business world, winning is a team sport. The same is true in our personal lives. Committed relationships result from collaboration—give and take, a two-way street. In chapter four I shared that one of my core values is intentional listening. I believe that the most vital component in working together is listening.

Hearing is passive. We hear a phone ring, the dryer tumble, or a siren wail.

Listening is active. It's when we give our undivided attention to another person.

Take a few minutes to think about who the *investors* in your life are, the people in your inner circle. They're on the inside because they're positive, uplifting, constructive, and healing. They're on the inside because you authentically connect with them; there's interaction; there's involvement; there's synergy.

No involvement means no commitment—no exception. For business and personal relationships to flourish, we must engage with the people in our lives. Together is better. Together is how we win.

It's been said that love makes the world go round. I believe that *communication*, not love, is what makes the world go round.

Self-expression is the seat of communication, the desire to convey personal feelings, ideas, beliefs, and concerns to others. One of the strongest human longings is to be heard and acknowledged. This need is deeply anchored to our connection with others.

Healthy communication is the ability to convey our thoughts, opinions, beliefs, and convictions in effective ways. What we say is an audible extension of what we think and how we feel, including the ability to disagree with others, voice views that are unpopular, and stand up for what we believe is right—all in a positive, non-destructive way.

> "Words are singularly the most powerful force available to humanity. We can choose to use this force constructively with words of encouragement, or destructively using words of despair. Words have energy and power with the ability to help, to heal, to hinder, to hurt, to harm, to humiliate, and to humble."
>
> —**YEHUDA BERG,** prominent authority on Kabbalah
> and author

People who are adept at healthy communication exercise front-end consideration before speaking. They express themselves without being overly defensive, arrogant, or aggressive. Not interrupting, they show respect for the other person by letting them finish what they're saying before they speak. I keep a postcard with this acronym visible in my office:

THINK before you speak.
T—Is it true?
H—Is it helpful?
I—Is it inspiring?
N—Is it necessary?
K—Is it kind?

Excellent communicators make eye contact with the other person and take in what they're saying. They give visual clues and utilize encouraging expressions of agreement—nodding their head, smiling, softly saying "uh-huh"—to let the other person know that they're actively listening.

Simple yet effective, we can cultivate a positive change in the behavior of those around when we use positive language by asking for what we want instead of stating what we don't want:

"Please remember to stop for milk" instead of "Don't forget the milk."
"Please shut the door quietly" instead of "Don't slam the door."

"Certainly," "great," and "definitely," are examples of affirmative statements that encourage and help develop neural pathways in the brain for positive thinking. They put a positive spin on our interaction with the people in our sphere of influence, people whose lives we touch, leaving an indelible imprint.

"It's interesting what happens when we use words purposefully and not reflexively."

—**CRISTEN IRIS**, editor, writer, book and business coach

Mountain or Molehill? It's a Matter of Balance

I balance my checkbook. I have my tires balanced. I strive for work-life balance. I do my best to eat a nutritionally balanced diet, and through the day I have a graceful dance partner—equilibrium—that keeps me physically balanced.

Like riding a bicycle, it's not too difficult to keep tangible, exterior things in balance once we learn how. It's those pesky intangibles, interior things, like stress or fear, where achieving balance can be like herding cats—feels next to impossible.

As you're reading this you might be organizing a bevy of items on an ever-growing *ta-dah* list: an overflowing email box, bills to pay, groceries to buy, dry cleaning to pick up, kids to drop off, calls to return. And every time you check an item off the list it seems to grow two more. So, you probably know experientially what I mean.

When life is out of balance, what would normally be molehills can seem like mountains. Not balance as in equilibrium, but feeling out of balance all day—every day—and never being still long enough to recharge our personal battery, to stabilize.

In school we learn that the strength of any structure depends on the greatest load applied to it, not exceeding its given limits. This strength and stability are derived through balance.

And so it is with humans. Instead of cement foundations and steel beams, one of our greatest supports is stillness, not necessarily the lack of motion.

Stillness is dynamic; it's un-conflicted movement—no friction. It can be experienced whenever there is total, unrestricted, participation in the moment, when we're unreservedly present with whatever we're doing. It's in stillness that I've come to understand that I can do anything, just not everything.

Imbalance is an indicator that something's got to go, that we need to offload ballast—people, places, and things—that keep us topsy-turvy. These might include extensive family obligations, a relationship that's bankrupting our heart, spending more than we earn, embracing beliefs that aren't true (e.g., "I'm not attractive" or "I'm not good enough"), or chasing unrealistic goals.

It's been said that our ability to be productive is directly proportional to our ability to relax—to be still. This includes making time to go within and work on our internal landscape, to till the garden of our heart and pull mental, emotional, or spiritual weeds, cultivating serenity even in the midst of chaos.

The Flip Side of Knowing

Twentieth-century science is known for three main theories: quantum mechanics, relativity, and chaos. The third one—chaos—is an umbrella theory that's wide brushstroke covers math, physics, biology, finance, and even music.

But what about mental, emotional, physical, and spiritual chaos? What about chaos in our homes, in our relationships, in our jobs?

In most instances, chaos can be attributed to unanswered questions. I refer to this as the *What If Factor*: What if he or she doesn't love me? What if I lose my job? What if I don't lose ten pounds by the date of the event? What if I get caught? What if no one cares?

Getting to the source that triggers the unanswered questions— the *What if Factor*—eliminates the need to know.

Divided into two hemispheres, the left side of the brain oversees mental activities such math and science while the right side is responsible for creative expression and intuitive functioning. Both sides store information. Data retrieval is referred to as *knowing*.

In a conversation, my friend Cassie shared, "I'm working on unknowing what I believe I know." Her comment brought to mind the wisdom of the bumper sticker that says, "Don't believe everything you think."

The world—especially in this Information Age—places great value on what we know. However, there's a tremendous interaction between knowing and not knowing, and they're both important. Just as the ability for knowing can be developed, so can the practice of not-knowing.

In his book *The Issue at Hand: Essays on Buddhist Mindfulness Practice*, author Gil Fronsdal says, "The Zen practice of not-knowing is sometimes referred to as 'beginner's mind'—seeing with fresh, unbiased eyes; not being blinded to new possibilities or preconceived ideas or judgments."

Any belief worth embracing should be able to stand up to scrutiny. If not, it's time to release it; let it go.

Adding "I don't know" to our thoughts is a healthy habit that helps us question our line of thinking, helps us examine the validity of our thoughts and tightly held beliefs. It creates a space for stillness in our mind—stillness that calms inner chaos.

Not-knowing doesn't mean information poverty; it doesn't mean that we're lost, bewildered, or uncertain. Nor does it mean that we have to overlook or ignore our understanding of a situation. Not-knowing means not being limited by what we do know.

When we hold the space of not-knowing, the limiting walls of certainty collapse revealing unlimited potential and possibility.

The practice of not-knowing is a conscious choice. By holding lightly to what we know, we're ready for it to be different. Maybe things are this way, but maybe, just maybe, they're not. . .

> "Peace. It does not mean to be in a place where there is no noise, trouble, or hard work. It means to be in the midst of those things and still be calm in our heart."
>
> **—UNKNOWN**

SECTION TWELVE

Financial Analysis

La Mandarine Bleue

Course Twelve—*Café*

Show Me the Money

Financial Analysis

"Doing good business—being ethical, being transparent, being caring, implementing values in your business—makes a difference, and you make money at the same time."

—**SHARI ARISON,** businesswoman, philanthropist, owner of Arison Investments, and Israel's wealthiest woman

Typically found at the end of a business plan, the financial component is crucial because it determines if a business is viable, if it's successful. But what is success? In the business world, it's typically monetary gain—revenue, profit.

In our personal lives, if you ask ten people to define success, you're likely to receive ten different answers. Why? Because we use different measuring tools.

My personal definition of success is *fulfillment*. The added bonus is that a person who's fulfilled sleeps well at night and wakes up refreshed.

But what about money as a measure of success?

Prosperity is material wealth; it's something that brings a return value to the wallet or bank account. It's external and has tangible dividends. You can touch it, hold it, drive it, live in it, wear it, swim in it, take it to the bank, or invest it. Examples include money, jewelry, real estate, cars, boats, recreational vehicles, collections, and investments.

A business may be funded or non-funded. If it's funded, the stake-holders expect an ROI—return on investment. We owe them a tangible, monetary profit. This falls under the prosperity category.

Abundance is inner wealth; it's something that brings a return value to the heart. It benefits our inner landscape with intangible dividends. Examples include love, peace of mind, health, wellness, wisdom, integrity, quality relationships, joy, gratitude, humor, a positive attitude, and contentment—being satisfied, being fulfilled.

In our personal lives, we have investors, too. These individuals are up close and personal, the people who love us. They deserve a return on their investment with non-tangibles such as love, respect, loyalty. These fall under the abundance category.

Interestingly, a person can be abundant and not prosperous, or a person can be prosperous and not abundant. A person can be both abundant and prosperous, or they can be neither. If you believe like I do that giving and receiving are the same then you understand that prosperity can be turned into abundance. An example of this is when a person shares or gives from their prosperity.

In terms of abundance, are you operating in the black—do you have a surplus? Or are you operating in the red—do you have a deficit?

Terrill Welch author of *Leading Raspberry jam Visions Women's Way: An Inside Track for Women Leaders* has this to say about success: "My challenge for us is to question all measures attributed to success—not just those that are beyond the quick and easy definition provided by wealth and position.

"I ask that we embrace the multiplicity of success, and carefully explore and articulate what we believe is success in a particular situation and also what consequences result from that success.

"For me, success is not about getting it right and sailing to the finish line of life. Success is about allowing your persistence to sail your vision through every day. . . while the breeze of your passion and potential charts your course."

1. How do you define success?
2. What are your measuring tools?
3. Based on your definition, how do you measure up; are you successful?

In the business world, we have tools to measure success. The term "keeping the books," refers to maintaining the general ledger—the main accounting record of business. It documents a company's lifetime of financial transactions.

It's comprised of three parts:

○ *Income Statement*—shows revenues, expenses, and profit for a particular period. It's a snapshot of whether or not the business is profitable at a specific point in time. The formula is: revenue - expenses = profit/loss.

○ *Cash Flow Projection*—shows how funds are expected to flow and informs of expenditures that are too high or when there's a surplus.

○ *Balance Sheet*—shows a picture of the business net worth at a particular point in time. It's a summary of the financial data broken into three categories: assets, liabilities, and equity.

In his book *Take the Stairs: 7 Steps to Achieving True Success*, author Rory Vaden states, "Success is never owned; it is only rented—and the rent is due every day." Business or personal, it's ongoing; it's day in and day out.

Never acceptable, double bookkeeping is when we're deceptive and then have to keep track of the deceit, the lie. At the office or in our home, in business or our personal lives, we have multiple touch points with others each day. Each of these is an opportunity to be honest, or not.

Aside from heartbreak of broken trust, the mental effort of double bookkeeping is extremely stressful. When we remember that ninety percent of all illness is stress related, we can safely deduce that there are negative consequences to the health and well-being of those who lie.

The benefits of being honest are many. A deeper, more complete honesty includes being true to ourselves and our purpose, fulfilling our potential, and expressing our gifts. This is where honesty becomes a spiritual practice, a path to peace, contentment, and fulfillment. Honesty is indeed the best policy.

To ensure financial health, a *good* business makes sure that shoe leather meets the street. A *great* business shakes hands and establishes an excellent rapport with existing and potential customers, developing relationships and building trust. The following list in and of itself isn't enough. It assumes that your product or service is exceptional.

- ○ Consistently visualize the end result.
- ○ Have a great attitude; wear an authentic smile.
- ○ Show up and do the work that needs to be done.
- ○ Know it will come true, but don't be attached to how.
- ○ Create an engaging monthly newsletter.
- ○ Care. Write a thank you note to someone daily, especially if it's not expected.
- ○ Connect with people in your industry.
- ○ Pay attention to people who mention your business online.
- ○ If someone stops using your product or service, find out why.
- ○ Facilitate classes for your customers.
- ○ Post a weekly blog that's not about promoting sales. Instead, provide nuggets of information readers can use.
- ○ Offer free samples at every opportunity.
- ○ Create a buyer/user guide that provides an honest shout-out to competitors where they do it better.
- ○ Sponsor industry events and host community meetings in your space.
- ○ Build a recruiting pipeline; stay in touch with people you used to work with.

The above-listed action items help to develop believability. Believability is embedded within the sales process from the first marketing action to earning the sale: follow through and follow-up.

Equally important are the details. When clients stepped through the doors of my brick and mortar facility, HolEssence, their senses were immediately engaged: their sense of smell was treated to our signature scent—a proprietary blend of essential oils; their sense of sight was gifted with soft lavender and dusty sage walls; and their hearing was delighted by soothing music. These details worked together to signal a softly spoken, subconscious, "Relax. You can let go now." Details serve to increase satisfaction.

- ❍ *Listen.* Ask Betty about her grandson, by name.
- ❍ *Care.* If you know a client's date of birth, send a birthday card.
- ❍ *Be kind.* Ask yourself, "What's it like to be on the receiving end of me?"
- ❍ *Take action.* Don't wait, take action now.
- ❍ *Practice excellence.* It's my opinion that each of us has an undeniable responsibility to ourselves and the rest of the world to be our personal best on any given day.
- ❍ *Play hard.* It will shine through in your work.

Play as a Spiritual Practice

In April of 2012, I had the unique opportunity to be one of eighty guests who enjoyed lunch with His Holiness the Dalai Lama at Loyola University after he spoke to a crowd of 4,000 people about the importance of non-violence and human compassion.

One of the things he shared was that he learns best when he laughs. Many of us have been taught that we must hold what is meaningful with a level of seriousness. So when it comes to spiritual matters, some of us take a more solemn approach, feeling that a playful connection with Spirit may disrespect that sacred experience.

Many spiritual traditions encourage us not to take ourselves too seriously. Remember Saint Francis of Assisi? His original followers were Angelus, a noble cavalier; Leo, the saint's secretary and confessor; Rufinus, a cousin of Saint Claire; and Saint Juniper, "the renowned jester of the Lord."

To our sensible selves, the antics of clowns and jesters may seem silly, but they have an important role—they carry the banner for play. Saint Francis said of Saint Juniper, "Would to God, my brothers, I had a whole forest of such Junipers." Our spirits need celebration. What feels joyful to us points us along the path to our personal growth and expansion.

> "You don't stop laughing because you grow old. You grow old because you stop laughing."
>
> —**MICHAEL PRITCHARD,** comedian

Play is the exuberant expression of our beings; it fuels our joy and wonder. Play provides the energetic space we need to feel alive; it taps into unlimited possibility, inspiring us. Play resides at the heart of our creativity and our most carefree moments of devotion; it's a powerful way to feed our soul.

It's been said that laughter is the best medicine, able to heal the body, mind, and soul. But in today's fast-paced world, many of us don't play enough. We're either too busy, too serious, or too predictable. The best remedy for these maladies is play.

When we relax the grip on our overflowing schedules and lengthy *ta-dah* lists, we find transformational space where we connect to our playful, creative, and inspirational selves, space that rings with laughter, space where we embrace our expansive selves, space where we welcome that which is divine.

You are cordially invited to shake hands with the lighter side of life, to play. *Tag—you're it!*

Living Your Legacy

If you lose your believability, you lose your credibility, and simultaneously your customer loses trust, and the chances of increased repeat business are significantly reduced.

In business or our personal lives, goodwill strengthens believability and credibility. What are you giving back to the community? If your goodwill were a pebble that was tossed into a still lake, how far would the ripple travel?

We all live different lives. We differ in perspective, age, gender, sexual orientation, ethnicity, culture, education, socioeconomic status, spiritual tradition, political views, interests, and lifestyles. That's what makes the world go round. But the one thing that levels the playing field, puts us all on the same page, is death. We're all going to die. You've seen the humorous bumper sticker. "Life: no one gets out alive."

How we face that fact and what we do with the time we're given is up to us individually. The culmination of our life experience is our legacy. Have you thought about what your legacy will be, what you'll be remembered for?

Legacy isn't necessarily about prosperity or leaving a sum of money to your children or grandchildren. It's about making a positive contribution while you're here. Your legacy—a lifetime of experience—is permanent and has a lasting impact. Whether it's your actions or inactions, the words you say or leave unsaid, never underestimate the influence—positive or negative—you have on others.

A person's legacy can be likened to a painted work of art; some are large while others are small. Many large canvases are paper thin and not considered substantial while several smaller portraits are considered masterpieces. The importance of the end result is the quality, not the size. What does your legacy look like?

If you're authentically living your purpose then by design you'll be a magnet for abundance. You may not be wealthy, but your life will indeed be rich. And your legacy—the culmination of your life experience—will be one of true and lasting value.

"A lot of ideas sound great on paper and even in discussions. However, simple math can make or break an idea. Before we launch any new idea, we at least create a financial model to project the ROI from several realistic scenarios. You can save a lot of time and frustration thinking through the numbers, and making sure it's possible to hit your revenue and profit goals."

—**PHIL FROST,** founder and COO of Main Street ROI

La Mandarine Bleue

"A recipe has no soul. You, as the cook, must bring soul to
the recipe."

—**THOMAS KELLER,** chef, restauranteur, and
cookbook author

It was mid-April and hummingbirds had arrived on the
scene two weeks before, easily reestablishing their pattern of zipping
and diving between the hand-blown glass feeders Dwayne and Larry
had strategically placed around the garden and deck.

"How often do you have to refill the feeders?" Élise asked.

"Because they're small, they empty fast, so I end up changing them
out daily. But that's good because it gives me the opportunity to keep
them clean," Dwayne answered.

The annual Garden Gathering Celebration took place just after Tax
Day. The other *La Mandarine Bleue* owners were continually grateful for
Bill's bookkeeping savvy and their accountant who verified that their Is
were dotted and Ts were crossed, and ensured that their taxes were paid
in a timely and accurate fashion.

"I propose a toast to our number crunchers," Peter said. "To Bill our
bookkeeper, Pat our accountant, and Heath our financial advisor. We
value your professional expertise and guidance. Thank you for everything you do on our behalf."

"A bientôt—cheers!" rang out startling even the bravest humming-birds, which dove behind the vibrant, two-toned red and white salvia "hot lips" flowers.

Pat raised her glass in response, "It's hard to believe America was founded, in part, to avoid high taxation."

Heath bantered back, "The wealth of experience is one possession that hasn't been taxed. . . yet."

Bill couldn't resist joining the fun, "Even if money could buy happiness, just think what the luxury tax would be! All kidding aside," he continued, "we've had another excellent year, and I believe it's because of our value proposition. We made a promise to ourselves and our customers, and we've kept it."

Both men smiling, Henri helped Larry carry food-laden trays to the back deck. Larry said, "Let's see if we can recite our mission/vision statement by heart. If we can, then we get to enjoy Cognac Shrimp with *Beurre Blanc* Sauce, couscous, and red pepper bean salad."

Without skipping a beat, Sally started, "*La Mandarine Bleue* is committed to an authentic French kitchen, cuisine, and wine. To satisfy parties of every size, our menu includes communal dishes as well as individual choices."

Dwayne continued, "Our dedication to service is exacting, yet our warm approach is welcoming and relaxed in a friendly, vibrant atmosphere."

Peter took the verbal baton, "We do this by consistently providing customers with timely, unintrusive service, demonstrating efficiency, knowledge, professionalism, and integrity in our work."

Yousef crossed the finish line with, "To ensure fresh, satisfying meals, our seasonally-driven menu is sourced locally whenever possible. Dining at *La Mandarine Bleue* isn't simply a meal; it's an experience."

All eyes turned to the center table where Henri and Larry had set the food trays down. "Oh my gosh, that looks delicious!" Sally said. Leaning forward and inhaling deeply, she added, "And it smells heavenly."

"Before we start, let's not forget our goals," Amina said. "To live our core values and be our personal best every day."

While everyone dished up, Sheila asked the group, "Have you seen the Blue Apron commercial on television? It asks, 'What if we could bring you better value by having better values?' It's that brilliant line of thinking that's made *La Mandarine Bleue* what it is today. Which brings up our core values. Do you think we can do as well reciting those by heart?"

Bill answered, "That's a great segue, Sheila. We've been asked for an interview by *Idaho* magazine and the question 'To what do you attribute your success?' invariably comes up. The answer's easy. From the beginning, the original team and every person hired after that has never lost sight of *La Mandarine Bleue's* core values: respect, excellence in hospitality, cultural authenticity, teamwork and family, social and ecological responsibility, and economic sustainability. And as Amina said, each of us is dedicated to living those core values and being our personal best every day."

"On the topic of being in print," Dwayne waggled his eyebrows at Élise and Henri, "my publisher doesn't publish cookbooks but has suggested a publisher for you to pitch a *La Mandarine Bleue* cookbook to." He finished with a half-bow flourish.

Verbal pandemonium erupted on the deck. "That's fantastic!" "Oh, my word!" "What a great idea!" "It'll be a best-seller!"

"I remember the first time we met to discuss opening a restaurant," Sally reminisced. "Bill, discerning businessman that he is, grilled us with every scenario he could think of about why it wouldn't work, testing our stamina with pointed questions, checking our financial acumen. When it was all said and done he shook our hands and said, 'I'm in, what do you need me to do?'"

"That seems ages ago." Bill laughed. "But it's only been three years. Three *extremely* good years. I believe that part of our success is directly attributable to our charitable work. That and the fact that we source as locally as possible, as sustainably as possible, and we're not caught in bias and fixed ideas. Instead, we're flexible in our thinking."

Sally added, "And we don't have a top down, totem pole hierarchy. The fact that we're free to exercise creativity and joy adds to the positive vibe our customers are drawn to."

Zoe voiced her thoughts out loud. "Individually and collectively we opened ourselves up to possible failure and as a result, probable success. We're fortunate that in our case we've met with and shake hands daily with, success. I'm grateful that we share our bounty with others, not only through food donations but with the financial contributions we make to those in need."

"On a side note," Amina added, "after our group outing to enjoy the historic downtown Boise food and cultural walking tour, I'm glad we've decided to approach them and suggest *La Mandarine Bleue* be included. We're a perfect fit! Plus, it would give us even more visibility."

The day had ended. Spring twilight had fallen like a soft cloth across the deck, the lawn, and over the limbs of the budding trees. Over steaming cups of *Café Français*, Larry said, "Using a passage from Ruth Picardie's *Before I Say Goodbye*, I'd like to propose a toast:

"What I wish for you is the same as for myself, a life, however short or long, that is as happy as possible and a death, however near or far, that is peaceful."

"*A bientôt*—cheers!"

Course Twelve—*Café*

Pronounced "kah-fay," this is the final course, the coffee course.

Café Français—French Coffee

Serves 4

Ingredients
- 4 ounces Cointreau® orange liqueur
- 2 oz Kahlua® coffee liqueur
- 20 ounces hot, black coffee
- 6 ounces whipped cream
- 4 teaspoons sugar
- 4 teaspoons Cointreau® orange liqueur

Preparation
Pour coffee, Cointreau®, and Kahlua® into an Irish coffee cup and sweeten to taste. Gently float the cream on top, add a teaspoon of Cointreau®, and serve.

Show Me the Money

"It's the intelligent thing to be frugal."

—CHUCK FEENEY, businessman, philanthropist, and
founder of The Atlantic Philanthropies, one of the
largest private foundations in the world

For a moment, think of yourself as a business. In our personal lives, establishing and maintaining a financial budget is the counterpart of financial analysis in the business arena.

Financial stress is widespread and growing. Concerns and anxiety over bills, debt, mortgages, interest rates, late fees, and other financial hardships are the leading cause of stress for Americans.

"The average US household credit card debt stands at $16,140, counting only those households carrying debt."[1] And, "Based on an analysis of Federal Reserve statistics and other government data, the average household owes $7,529 on their cards; looking only at indebted households, the average outstanding balance rises to $16,140. Current as of October 2015, here is the US household consumer debt profile:

- Average credit card debt: $16,140
- Average mortgage debt: $155,361
- Average student loan debt: $31,946"[2]

Finances cover a broad spectrum, from shaky and unstable to secure and steady. Regardless, our financial position has a large impact on our emotional outlook.

Spendthrift and Pennywise

In my book *Note to Self: A Seven-Step Path to Gratitude and Growth,* I use two fictional characters to discuss personal finances.

Spendthrift operates from a weak financial position. They put little thought into their spending habits. Consequently, they're overextended financially.

Spendthrift hasn't planned for the future. They haven't saved any money for their retirement years. If they were to lose their job unexpectedly, they wouldn't have enough savings to tide them over for long—one to two months, perhaps.

Spendthrift is the type of person who bases their expenditures on what they want as opposed to what they need. Sometimes they buy things just for the sake of having them. Maybe it's to keep up with the Joneses; maybe it's to keep up with themselves.

Often, Spendthrift charges items they can't otherwise afford. They put their purchases on a credit card and end up paying interest because they don't have the ability to pay off their card at the end of every month.

By struggling to live within their means, Spendthrift adds weight to their life's baggage and minimizes their joy.

Pennywise operates from a strong financial position. They're thoughtful in their spending habits. More accurately, they're thoughtful in their saving habits. Consequently, they aren't overextended financially.

Pennywise has planned for the future. They've saved money for their retirement years. If Pennywise were to lose their job unexpectedly, they'd have enough savings set aside to tide them over for a long time—long enough for them to find another job.

Pennywise is the type of person who bases their expenditures on what they need first. They don't buy things for the sake of having them. When they do find something they want, they may use their charge card to earn air miles or other types of incentives, but they always pay their card off at the end of every month.

If Pennywise can't afford it, Pennywise doesn't buy it. They don't carry a balance on their charge card, so they never incur interest fees.

Pennywise lives within their means, making more money than they spend.

My client Nadine is the epitome of Pennywise. Her philosophy is, "The less we have, the more room we have to live right-sized lives." The "less is more" attitude adds exponentially to her joy factor.

Skinny Cow to Cash Cow

If you're not a prime candidate for using a credit card—paying it off at the end of every month like Pennywise—then you've got the option to become a **cash cow**!

A cash cow is responsible for a significant portion of a company's profit. Every business longs for a cash cow product.

In your personal life, you become a cash cow by ditching your credit cards and using cash instead. It's easy!

Establish an envelope for each type of expense: groceries, clothing, gasoline, etc. And remember to include an envelope for "grin" money, a small amount of personal money to spend any way you'd like.

A savvy budgeter bears in mind that their income must be greater than their outgo. Determine how much you can spend in each category. Then go to the ATM, or make a check out to "Cash" and request fives, tens, and twenty dollar bills. When you return home, divide the money into the respective envelopes.

Your gasoline budget, for example, may be fifty dollars a week ($200/month). On the front of the envelope write "Gasoline $200."

When you go to the grocery store, write the date, how much you spent, and the remaining amount like you would in your checkbook register. This visual will help keep you on track and allow you to see your monthly progress.

Don't spend more than the weekly amount you allotted. If you do then next week you'll have less to spend. Some months you may have precious little money left. This is referred to as "too much month at the end of the money."

When this happens, it usually serves as a *spring housecleaning* tool, ensuring that everything gets used: peanut butter, soup, ramen noodles, rice and beans, fruits and vegetables.

Using cash envelopes is an effective way to control spending, and it instills discipline and keeps you within budget.

Right-Sizing My Life

When my husband and I relocated from Illinois to the Pacific Northwest in the spring of 2014, we shifted gears from an already small home we'd lived in for over twenty years to a simple 600-square-foot carriage house. People often ask us, "Why on earth would you choose to downsize?" The reasons are simple.

First, I think of it as right-sizing—right for us—not downsizing. Empty-nesters in our fifties, now is the time to work less, travel more, live debt free, and do the things we want. For us, the intentional promotion of our greatest passions (for me it's writing, for my husband it's flying) and the removal of everything that distracts us from them, has been liberating.

We intentionally live below our means so we can travel. The less we spend, the more we save. The more we save, the more we can pursue our co-interest—travel—and additionally not worry about our retirement years.

Second, we live in an area that we wouldn't otherwise be able to afford. Nestled between the shoulders of distinctive mansions rich with heritage in one of the historic districts in Boise, the carriage house we live in (circa 1865) is the oldest, still-standing structure in the town that was founded as the "City of Trees" in 1863.

Another question we hear when the topic of downsizing comes up is, "What did you do with all of your stuff?" We donated most of our items to a woman's shelter, but we know other downsizers who had yard sales and sold items on eBay and Craigslist. Then they used those funds to pay off their debt. Like many others, we found it liberating to offload baggage that weighed us down.

A smaller home means less space. Having eliminated the unnecessary, we are deliberate and thoughtful about the few things we do have. Implementing the adage, "a place for everything and everything in its place," the shift has forced me to become an Organizational Goddess! One example is the use of bed risers. I increased our under-bed storage by using bed lifts. We store off-season clothes in airtight containers in space that would otherwise collect dust bunnies. Living in less space means we spend less time, stress, and money on upkeep.

As a transformational life coach, I've had many clients tell me that instead of being homeowners, they feel owned by their homes. Between the mortgage payment, insurance, taxes, and maintenance, they find themselves financially strapped. The most recent census data reveals that the average new single-family home comes in at just under 2,600 square feet. That may not sound significant but a look back shows us that in 1950 the average family home size was less than 1,000 square feet.

Is downsizing, right-sizing, simplifying, or minimalism right for everyone? I think it's different for individuals, couples, and families of varying configurations. The two things about downsizing that are probably the most off-putting are: "What if I need this later?" and "I can't part with this because of its sentimental value." Here's what we found.

We save so much money by shedding—not storing—the "what if I need it later" items, that if we do discover a need for it, we re-buy it, and then donate it when we're done using it. In the two years since we relocated, we haven't yet had to repurchase anything we gave away.

I had several photo albums that I thought I couldn't part with. Because of today's technology, I was able to photograph the photos and upload them into digital albums. I also photographed items that had sentimental value (you know, the ones that are boxed in the garage attic) and then donated them. I haven't looked at those photos any more than I ever climbed into the attic to admire those sentimental items—never.

Embracing the belief that life is an expression of the choices we make, I'm a teacher and student of purposeful living. With tremendous respect for the earth's natural resources, my goal is to leave the slightest footprint on the planet while at the same time making a lasting impression on its inhabitants—one that is positive, uplifting, constructive, and healing.

How would you answer the following questions?

1. Are your financial habits more like Spendthrift's, more like Pennywise's, or somewhere in between?

2. Are you satisfied with what you have, or are you more concerned with what you don't have yet?
3. Do you have a written budget where you've listed your income and all of your expenses and calculated the difference?
4. Do you live within your means, or do you spend more money than you earn?

One of the best books I've ever read about establishing a budget and financial planning is Julie Murphy Casserly's *The Emotion Behind Money: Building Wealth from the Inside Out*. If you feel overwhelmed at the idea of creating a personal budgeting plan, this easy-to-read and enjoyable book offers a foolproof way to create, organize, and maintain a personal budget. It's a step-by-step guide to getting yourself on track financially and staying there for the rest of your life.

Creating a financial budget is establishing a boundary. But to be effective, the boundary must be maintained. Establishing and maintaining boundaries are two different things.

Establishing a boundary is defining it and setting it in place.

Maintaining a boundary is weaving it into your lifestyle and checking it often to ensure that it holds.

Establish a solid, realistic financial plan and follow it. Doing so goes a long way toward ensuring that you won't run out of money before you run out of years. A boundary is effective only if it's maintained.

"A minimalist by intent, I live a beautiful life with few things—simple, yet full."

—**LAURIE BUCHANAN,** holistic health practitioner, transformational life coach, and author

Conclusion

"It is good to have an end to journey toward, but it is the journey that matters in the end."

—URSULA K. LE GUIN, author

It's imperative that we walk our talk. At home or in the office, if our values are important enough to express, they're important enough to live by.

In the business world, revenue is the bottom line. If a company has clearly defined and is incorporating—*living*—the principles outlined in this book, they're much more likely to operate in the black.

In our personal lives, profit includes peace of mind, joy of heart, and health. If a person has clearly defined and is incorporating—*living*—the principles outlined in this book, the dividends multiply with a ripple effect that includes active gratitude and kindness.

Business or personal, everyone has an important story. But sometimes we get caught in one point of view—our perspective—and can't see the bigger picture. I never fail to be inspired by the following story about adversity and perspective. The author (unknown) is clearly a wise soul.

Carrots, Eggs, and Coffee

A young woman went to her mother and told her about her life and how things were so hard for her. She did not know how she was going to make it and wanted to give up. She was tired of fighting and struggling. It seemed that as one problem was solved a new one arose.

Her mother took her to the kitchen. She filled three pots with water. In the first, she placed carrots, in the second she placed eggs, and the last she placed ground coffee beans.

She let them sit and boil without saying a word. In about twenty minutes she turned off the burners. She fished the carrots out and placed them in a bowl. She pulled the eggs out and placed them in a bowl. Then she ladled the coffee into a bowl. Turning to her daughter, she asked, "Tell me what you see?"

"Carrots, eggs, and coffee," she replied.

She brought her closer and asked her to feel the carrots. She did and noted that they were soft. She then asked her to take an egg and break it. After pulling off the shell, she observed the hard-boiled egg. Finally, she asked her to sip the coffee. The daughter smiled, as she tasted its rich aroma.

The daughter then asked, "What's the point, mother?"

Her mother explained that each of these objects had faced the same adversity, boiling water, but each reacted differently:

The carrot went in strong, hard, and unrelenting. However, after being subjected to the boiling water, it softened and became weak.

The egg had been fragile. Its thin outer shell had protected its liquid interior. But, after being through the boiling water, its inside became hardened.

The ground coffee beans were unique, however. After they had been in the boiling water, they had changed the water.

"Which are you?" she asked the daughter. "When adversity knocks on your door, how do you respond? Are you a carrot, egg, or a coffee bean?"

How about you?

Are you like the carrot that appears strong, but loses its strength when faced with adversity?

Are you like the egg that starts with a soft heart but hardens with the heat?

Or are you like the coffee bean? It released its essence into the boiling water.

If you're like the coffee bean, when things are at their worst you change the situation around you.

Be the bean!

"To laugh often and much; to win the respect of intelligent people and the affection of children; to earn the appreciation of honest critics and endure the betrayal of false friends; to appreciate beauty; to find the best in others; to leave the world a bit better, whether by a healthy child, a garden patch or a redeemed social condition; to know even one life has breathed easier because you have lived. This is to have succeeded."

—RALPH WALDO EMERSON, poet, lecturer, and essayist

Acknowledgments

Thank you to all the coworkers, managers, and mentors I've worked with over the years. I've learned something and benefited from each one of you.

Thank you to my sharp-eyed editor Cristen Iris. Slaying grammatical dragons—including my superfluous use of em dashes—was the least of your challenges. I'm grateful for your sense of humor and fiercely productive availability.

My heartfelt thanks to the team of professionals at She Writes Press and BookSparks. Your subject matter expertise is incomparable. I appreciate your commitment to publishing, promoting, and getting this book into the hands of readers.

Thank you to UW-Madison Writers' Institute for hosting three decades of engaging guest instructors who generously share actionable tips, techniques, and information in their sessions; with a special nod to Laurie Scheer, Christine DeSmet, and Laura Kahl—*mon chapeau est hors de vous.*

Thank you to Laura and Bruce DeLaney, owners of Rediscovered Books in Boise, Idaho for your community involvement and unceasing support of writers. As noted in Nina George's novel *The Little Paris Bookshop,* "It is a common misconception that booksellers look after books. They look after people."

Thank you to my in-laws, Mary and Gerry Stacy, for gifting me with the opportunity to winter in your home to finish writing this book. Being surrounded by the jaw-dropping beauty of the Bitterroot Valley while you were Down Under was the opportunity of a lifetime.

I am grateful to my sister, Julie Hunter. I enjoyed our snow-laden escapades while we teased out and mulled over the ever-important details of this book. I will always remember our French luncheon adventure with great fondness—I'm still full!

Thank you to my husband, Len—stalwart champion of my work—for braving the treacherous Lost Trail Pass to visit me during my winter sabbatical in Big Sky Country to complete this book. Your insights always encourage me to up my game.

Notes

PREFACE

1. Fred Meyer, Inc.
http://www.encyclopedia.com/social-sciences-and-law/economics-business-and-labor/businesses-and-occupations/fred-meyer-inc

2. "A Better Way to Say 'I'm Retired'"
https://www.forbes.com/sites/nextavenue/2017/01/10/a-better-way-to-say-im-retired/#59c1e8a07c7b

3. "Jubilee"
https://www.merriam-webster.com/dictionary/jubilee

SECTION ONE

1. "10 Reasons Why You Should Write a Business Plan"
https://smallbiztrends.com/2013/01/10-reasons-write-business-plan.html

2. Downtown Boise
http://pds.cityofboise.org/planning/hp/districts/

3. Commission for Libraries Literacy in the Park
http://libraries.idaho.gov/page/literacy-park

4. Warm Springs Avenue, Boise
http://pds.cityofboise.org/planning/hp/districts/

5. The North End, Boise
http://pds.cityofboise.org/planning/hp/districts/

6. Harrison Boulevard, Boise
http://pds.cityofboise.org/planning/hp/districts/

7. Ikigai
https://www.ted.com/talks/dan_buettner_how_to_live_to_be_100?
language=en

8. Compassion
https://www.psychologytoday.com/blog/the-compassion-chronicles/
200804/what-is-compassion-and-how-can-it-improve-my-life

9. John Mertz
https://www.thindifference.com/2010/11/my-personal-philosophy/

10. Oprah Winfrey
https://www.forbes.com/sites/quora/2011/11/29/what-is-a-good-
summary-of-oprahs-philosophy-of-life/#5001ddc029f2

11. Apolo Ohno
https://theinkwellonline.com/2017/02/09/athletes-express-their-
love-for-sports/

12. "Boundary"
https://www.merriam-webster.com/dictionary/boundary

SECTION TWO

1. Eric Jacobson
http://fortune.com/2015/03/13/company-slogans/

2. Nike
http://about.nike.com

3. Krispy Kreme
https://www.krispykreme.com/About/Our-Story

4. Sounds True
http://www.soundstrue.com/store/about-us/our-vision

5. Disney
http://www.entrepreneurshipinabox.com/3507/12-mission-statements-worth-checking/

6. Ford
http://corporate.ford.com/company.html

7. Avon
http://www.avoncompany.com/aboutavon/index.html

8. Aon Hewitt
http://www.aonhewitt.gr/en/AboutHewitt/WhoWeAre/index.html

9. Make-A-Wish Foundation
http://wish.org/about-us/our-story/ourmission#sm.00016kowab6gsembr2l1oo2r7qon3

10. Starbucks
https://www.starbucks.com/about-us/company-information/mission-statement

11. Ben & Jerry's
http://www.benjerry.com/values

12. Whole Foods Market
http://www.wholefoodsmarket.com/mission-values

13. Ninety-Nines
https://www.ninety-nines.org

14. Apple
http://www.newyorker.com/news/news-desk/steve-jobs-technology-alone-is-not-enough

15. Tim Cook, Apple
http://www.businessinsider.com/cook-update-jobs-famous-mission-statement-2016-6

16. Microsoft
https://www.microsoft.com/en-us/about/default.aspx

17. Laurie Buchanan
https://tuesdayswithlaurie.com/about-speaking-from-the-heart/

18. Volkswagen
http://www.volkswagen-me.com/en-vwme/volkswagen/fleet/volkswagen-mission-statement.html

19. AirBnB
http://blog.airbnb.com/fighting-discrimination-and-creating-a-world-where-anyone-can-belong-anywhere/

20. Facebook
https://www.facebook.com/pg/facebook/about/

21. Tara Darrow, Nordstrom
http://fortune.com/2015/03/13/company-slogans/

22. Google
http://fortune.com/2016/06/23/fortune-500-best-workplaces/

23. Janet Givens
http://janetgivens.com/about-the-author/

SECTION THREE

1. Safety
https://7geese.com/benefits-of-having-core-values-and-how-to-set-them-in-your-organization/

2. "The Trader Joe's Way for Libraries"
https://informationactivist.com/2013/11/27/the-trader-joes-way-for-libraries-a-manifesto-part-iii/

3. Coca-Cola Mission, Vision, and Values
http://www.coca-colacompany.com/our-company/mission-vision-values

4. Hewlett-Packard Values and Objectives
http://www.hp.com/hpinfo/abouthp/values-objectives.html

5. Sounds True Core Values
http://www.soundstrue.com/store/about-us/core-values

6, 7, 8, 9, and 10. "Make Your Values Mean Something"
https://hbr.org/2002/07/make-your-values-mean-something

11. Strategic Discipline Blog
http://strategicdiscipline.positioningsystems.com/bid/87326/Jim-Collins-or-Patrick-Lencioni-s-Vision-of-Core-Values

12. "Is Gratitude Good for You?"
https://www.psychologytoday.com/blog/evidence-based-living/201611/is-gratitude-good-you-0

13. "Thanksgiving: Gratitude at Home and at Work May Lead to a Longer, Happier Life"

https://www.forbes.com/sites/nealegodfrey/2016/11/20/thanksgiving-gratitude-at-home-and-at-work-may-lead-to-a-longer-happier-life/#65eddaa70639

14. "The Science of Gratitude"
http://moodwatchers.com/wp/?tag=gratitude-2&paged=2

SECTION FOUR

1. Coca-Cola Mission and Values
http://www.coca-colacompany.com/our-company/mission-vision-values

2. "Success is Personal"
https://theinformationage.co/2016/12/29/success-is-personal/

3. "Top 10 New Year's Resolutions for 2012"
http://www.plazacollege.edu/top-10-new-years-resolutions-for-2012-what-are-your-new-years-resolutions/

4. "How to Keep Your New Year's Resolutions"
http://www.newsobserver.com/news/business/article123024894.html

5. "One Key to Happiness? Failure."
http://www.heathershumaker.com/blog/2013/11/06/one-key-to-happiness-failure/

6. "Steve Jobs on the Remarkable Power of Asking for Help"
https://www.inc.com/peter-economy/steve-jobs-on-the-remarkable-power-of-asking-for-what-you-want.html

SECTION FIVE

1. Nokia
http://managementstudyguide.com/marketing-segmentation-targeting-positioning.htm

2. Ethics and Social Responsibility
http://www.igi-global.com/article/target-marketing-ethics-brand-advertising/47393

3. R. J. Reynolds Tobacco Company
http://www.nytimes.com/1990/01/12/business/a-cigarette-campaign-under-fire.html

4. Enron
https://www.forbes.com/sites/kensilverstein/2013/05/14/enron-ethics-and-todays-corporate-values/#7fe94e695ab8

5. Tyco
http://www.nbcnews.com/id/9399803/ns/business-corporate_scandals/t/ex-tyco-executives-get-years-prison/#.WPTw51LMzow

6. WorldCom
http://www.cbsnews.com/news/world-class-scandal-at-worldcom/

7. Bernie Madoff
http://nypost.com/2015/01/23/bernie-madoff-wracked-with-grief-over-unforgiving-sons/

8. Daniel Goleman
https://www.ted.com/talks/daniel_goleman_on_compassion

9. Forbes
https://www.forbes.com/2008/10/16/corporate-social-responsibility-corprespons08-lead-cx_mn_de_tw_1016csr_land.html

10. Fast Company
http://www.ehow.com/info_8516645_importance-ethics-marketing-segmentation.html

11. Personal Branding
https://en.wikipedia.org/wiki/Personal_branding

12. Glenn Llopis Group

http://www.digitalistmag.com/lob/human-resources/2015/06/26/
5-harsh-truths-better-leader-in-digital-age-02997432

SECTION SIX

1. "The Hypnotic Danger of Competitive Analysis" http://www.reference
forbusiness.com/small/Bo-Co/Competitive-Analysis.html

2. Mind-Your-Own-Business Plant
https://www.rhs.org.uk/advice/profile?pid=348

SECTION SEVEN

1. "Occupation"
https://www.merriam-webster.com/dictionary/occupation

2. Lee Clow
https://findingmastery.net/lee-clow/

3. "The Anatomy of a Really Good Résumé: A Good Résumé Example"
http://thevisualcommunicationguy.com/2014/06/19/the-anatomy-
of-a-really-good-resume-a-good-resume-example/

SECTION EIGHT

1. Ad Messages
http://www.nytimes.com/2007/01/15/business/media/15everywhere.
html?

2. "Starbucks and McDonald's Winning Strategy" https://www.forbes.com
/sites/panosmourdoukoutas/2013/04/25/starbucks-and-mcdonalds-
winning-strategy/#1f82d97aadb5

3. Ocean Medallion Technology
https://beyondphilosophy.com/case-study-enhance-cx-technology/

4. Oprah Winfrey
http://www.oprah.com/spirit/oprah-winfrey-on-her-new-show/all

5. Mentor Relationships
https://www.forbes.com/sites/ryanwestwood/2017/01/18/6-things-great-entrepreneurs-dont-do-that-set-them-apart-from-the-mediocre/#2169bc0e3889

6. Naikon
http://www.thesunmagazine.org/_media/article/pdf/348_Krech.pdf

SECTION NINE

1. "Consumer's Wants and Needs"
https://www.boundless.com/marketing/textbooks/boundless-market-ing-textbook/introduction-to-marketing-1/introduction-to-marketing-18/customer-wants-and-needs-107-4453/

2. Equip the Back Office
http://www.bain.com/publications/articles/is-complexity-killing-your-sales-model.aspx

3. Google's "Sweet Spot"
https://www.linkedin.com/pulse/using-googles-sweet-spot-create-standout-moments-colin-burcher

4. "New Business Models in Emerging Markets"
https://hbr.org/2011/01/new-business-models-in-emerging-markets

5. Reputation
https://www.psychologytoday.com/blog/happiness-in-world/201004/the-value-good-reputation

6. The Untrapped Mind
http://www.articlebiz.com/article/310513-1-the-untrapped-mind-in-40-words/

7. Newton's Third Law of Motion
http://www.physicsclassroom.com/class/newtlaws/lesson-4/newton-s-third-law

SECTION TEN

1. NBIA on Business Failure
http://www.moyak.com/papers/small-business-statistics.html

2. Product and Product Launches
https://www.forbes.com/sites/neilpatel/2015/03/16/8-elements-of-a-robust-product-launch-strategy/#49da6379220a

3. Process
http://www.insightsassociation.org/article/importance-process-new-product-development

4. Apple, Minimum Viable Product
https://www.forbes.com/sites/neilpatel/2015/03/16/8-elements-of-a-robust-product-launch-strategy/3/#4125e3363490

5. "Preparing for the Perfect Product Launch"
https://hbr.org/2007/04/preparing-for-the-perfect-product-launch

6. Product Launches and Change
https://www.forbes.com/sites/neilpatel/2015/03/16/8-elements-of-a-robust-product-launch-strategy/3/#45193d9c3490

7. "Lemonade Stand" Business Practices
http://www.huffingtonpost.com/stephanie-stclaire/11-things-i-wish-i-knew-when-i-started-my-business_b_9587398.html

8. Narcissus
http://www.theoi.com/Heros/Narkissos.html

9. "Narcissism"
http://www.dictionary.com/browse/narcissism

10. "Pizzled"
https://www.ted.com/talks/daniel_goleman_on_compassion

11. Outsourcing Our Lives
http://www.smh.com.au/comment/spend-time-not-money-and-dont-outsource-your-life-20151030-gkmpf7.html)

12. "Human Trash"
http://www.cnn.com/2014/05/01/opinion/selinger-outsourcing-activities/index.html

SECTION ELEVEN

1. Business Lies
https://www.linkedin.com/pulse/20141209145608-52594—everyone-is-replaceable-and-other-business-lies

2. Strong Leaders
https://www.linkedin.com/pulse/20141209145608-52594—everyone-is-replaceable-and-other-business-lies

3. Mindfulness
https://www.takingcharge.csh.umn.edu/what-mindfulness

4. Creating a Culture of Giving
https://youtu.be/YyXRYgjQXX0

5. Boise River, "The Wooded River"
http://boisemeridian.com/boise-is-waiting/

SECTION TWELVE

1. Credit Card Debt

http://nypost.com/2015/12/05/increased-credit-card-use-fuels-household-debt/

2. Student Loan Debt

http://pricewebss.pbworks.com/w/file/fetch/102028177/American%20Household%20Credit%20Card%20Debt%20Statistics.pdf

3. "Wabi-sabi"

https://en.wikipedia.org/wiki/Wabi-sabi

Glossary

Advertising: promoting the sale of products or services

Asset: a useful or valuable thing, person, or quality

Benchmark: a point of reference for evaluating a level of quality

Bistro: a Parisian-style restaurant that serves meals, wine, and coffee

(Business) Depth: the number of products or services available in each product line within a company

(Business) Width: the number of product lines available in a company's definition of offering

Business to Business (B2B): wholesale or retail trading between businesses

Cash Cow: a business, investment, or product that provides a steady income or profit

Core Values: principles that guide an organization's internal conduct and its relationship with the external world

Corporate Social Responsibility (CSR): demonstrating a concern for human rights, the environment, community development, and employee rights

Court of Public Opinion: using the news media to influence public support for one side or the other in a court case

Customer Experience (CX): the result of an interaction between an organization and a customer over the duration of their relationship

Customer Relationship Management (CRM): practices, strategies, and technologies used to manage and analyze customer interaction and data for the purpose of improving business relationships, assisting customer retention, and driving sales growth

Definition of Offering: the goods or services a company offers the public or other businesses. If a company offers more than one good or service, the offering is referred to as a *product mix*

Digital Footprint: the data left behind by users on digital services

Digital Native: a person familiar with technology from an early age

Due Diligence: reasonable steps taken by a person to satisfy legal requirements, especially when buying or selling something

Equity: the net difference when the total liabilities are subtracted from the total assets

Ethnography: the study of cultures where the researcher observes people from the subject's point of view

Foodie: a person with a particular interest in food; a connoisseur of good food; a person with a discerning palate

Gallic: French or typically French

Goals: the destination. Goals define where you are going and when you are going to arrive. Mission and vision statements, core values, and goals should tie into each other

Gross Domestic Product (GDP): a financial measure of the value of goods and services produced in a given period (quarterly or yearly)

Human Capital: the skills, knowledge, and experience possessed by an individual or population, viewed regarding their value or cost to an organization

Human Resources (HR): the department of a business or organization that deals with the hiring, administration, and training of personnel

Human Resource Management (HRM): a function in organizations designed to maximize employee performance in service of an employer's strategic objectives

Liability: a debt owed to a creditor of a company

Marketing Action Plan (MAP): a comprehensive blueprint that outlines an organization's overall marketing efforts

Market: two or more parties involved in a transaction of goods or services in exchange for money; the parties are known as sellers and buyers

Marketing: creating awareness of products or services

Market Segmentation: the process of dividing a total market into identifiable groups of people with similar needs

Market Targeting: locating a specific group of consumers at which a company aims its products and services

Management by Objectives (MBO) also known as Management by Results (MBR): a management model designed to improve an organization's performance by clearly defining objectives agreed to by both management and employees

Millennial: a person reaching young adulthood around the year 2000 (born between 1977–1998), also known as Generation Y

Minimum Viable Product (MVP): a product with the highest return on investment versus risk

Mission Statement: a brief statement that declares what a business or organization does

Monthly Recurring Revenue (MRR): the portion of a company's revenue that is highly likely to continue in the future; revenue that's predictable, stable, and can be counted on in the future with a high degree of certainty

Non-Governmental Organizations (NGO): any non-profit, voluntary citizens' group which is organized on a local, national, or international level

Niche: a specialized segment of the market for a particular kind of product or service

Objectives: the map. Objectives are the specific steps taken to reach the destination

Objectives and Key Results (OKRs): a technique for setting, communicating, and tracking, goals, objectives, and results in organizations

Panache: flamboyant confidence of style or manner

Personal Brand: how a person appears to the world

Private Sector: non-government employers including corporations, limited partnerships, and individual businesses

Public Sector: federal, state, and local government employers

Personal Value Proposition (PVP): the heart of a person's career strategy; it's what sets a person apart. It is the reason to hire you, not someone else

Prix-fixe: a meal consisting of several courses served at a total fixed price

Research and Development (R&D): work directed toward the innovation, introduction, and improvement of products and processes

Résumé: a brief account of one's professional or work experience and qualifications

Ripple Effect: a situation in which ripples flow outward across the water when an object is dropped into it

Return on Investment (ROI): the most common profitability ratio. There are several ways to determine ROI, but the most frequently used method is to divide net profit by total assets. So, if your net profit is $100,000 and your total assets are $300,000, your ROI would be .33 or 33 percent

Software as a Service (SaaS): a model where centrally-hosted software is licensed and delivered on a subscription basis, sometimes referred to as *on-demand software*

Securities and Exchange Commission (SEC): a US federal agency established to protect investors by setting mandatory standards for companies whose securities are traded on the stock exchange, and for enforcing securities-related laws

[*sic*]: "sic," used in brackets after a quoted word [*sic*] indicates that the passage has been retained in its original form

SMART Goals: Specific, Measurable, Attainable, Realistic, Time-bound

Sommelier: French word for a wine steward who is highly knowledgeable and trained in all aspects of wine

SWOT: Strengths, Weaknesses, Opportunities, and Threats

Talent Acquisition: the process of finding and acquiring skilled human labor for organizational needs to meet a job requirement

Unique Selling Proposition (USP) also known as Unique Selling Point: what a company has that its competitors don't

Value Centered: based on integrity

Value Proposition: a promise of value; the reason a target customer should buy a product or service

Vision Statement: a statement of what a company aspires to be

Zen Shin: an integrated approach to balanced health, living, and being, based on the recognition of our innate wholeness; some would say "being with what is"

Bibliography and Images

Adams, Scott. *How to Fail at Almost Everything and Still Win Big: Kind of the Story of My Life*. New York, NY: Portfolio, 2013.

Athmer, Kate, and Johnson, Rob. *Millennial Reboot: Our Generation's Playbook for Professional Growth*. Carson City, NV: Lioncrest Publishing LLC, 2016.

Buchanan, Laurie. *Note to Self: A Seven-Step Path to Gratitude and Growth*. Berkeley, CA: She Writes Press Inc., 2016.

Buechner, Frederick. *Wishful Thinking: A Seeker's ABC*. San Francisco, CA: HarperOne, 1993.

Burnett, Bill, and Evans, Dave. *Designing Your Life: How to Build a Well-Lived, Joyful Life*. New York, NY: Knopf Publishing Group, 2016.

Casserly, Julie Murphy. *The Emotion Behind Money: Building Wealth from the Inside Out*. Chicago, IL: Beyond Your Wildest Dreams LLC, 2008.

Coelho, Paul. The Alchemist. HarperOne. 2006.

Collins, Jim, and Porras, Jerry. *Built to Last: Successful Habits of Visionary Companies* (3rd edition). New York, NY: HarperBusiness, 2011.

DeGroot, Robert. *Objection Free Selling: How to Prevent, Preempt, and Respond to Every Sales Objection You Get.* Houston, TX: Sales Training International, 2016.

Frankl, Viktor E. *Man's Search for Meaning.* Boston, MA: Beacon Press, first published in 1946.

Forbes, David. *The Science of Why: Decoding Human Motivation & Transforming Marketing Strategy.* Palgroave Macmillan. 2015.

Fronsdal, Gil. *The Issue at Hand: Essays on Buddhist Mindfulness Practice.* Redwood City, CA: Insight Meditation Center, 2002.

Hamilton, Ryan, and Shaw, Colin. *The Intuitive Customer: 7 Imperatives For Moving Your Customer Experience to the Next Level.* Palgrave Macmillan, Basingstoke: UK, 2016.

Krech, Gregg. *Naikan: Gratitude, Grace, and the Japanese Art of Self-Reflection.* Berkeley, CA: Stone Bridge Press, 2001.

Lucas, James R. *Fatal Illusions: Shredding a Dozen Unrealities That Can Keep Your Organization From Success.* New York, NY: Amacom, 1997.

Marturano, Janice. *"Finding the Space to Lead: A Practical Guide to Mindful Leadership."* New York, NY: Bloomsbury Press, 2015.

Nourse, Kevin, and Schmidt, Lynn. *Shift Into Thrive: Six Strategies For Women to Unlock the Power of Resiliency.* Washington, DC: Bobo Publishing, 2016.

Picardie, Ruth. *Before I Say Goodbye.* Penguin UK. 1998.

Pressfield, Steven. *The War of Art: Break Through the Blocks and Win Your Inner Creative Battles.* Brooklyn, NY: Black Irish Entertainment LLC, November 2011.

Ries, Al, and Trout, Jack. *Positioning: The Battle for Your Mind*, 20th Anniversary Edition. Columbus, OH: McGraw-Hill Education, 2000.

Stein, Garth. *The Art of Racing in the Rain*. New York, NY: Harper, 2008.

Vaden, Rory. *Take the Stairs: 7 Steps to Achieving True Success*. TarcherPerigee, London: UK, February 2012.

Welch, Terrill. *Leading Raspberry Jam Visions Women's Way: An Inside Track for Women Leaders*. Vancouver, BC: Trafford Publishing, 2005.

IMAGES

The View Inside Me/What is Your Ikigai
http://theviewinside.me/what-is-your-ikigai/

Sweet Spot
https://www.linkedin.com/pulse/using-googles-sweet-spot-create-standout-moments-colin-burcher

About the Author

Board Certified by the American Association of Drugless Practitioners, **Laurie Buchanan** is a holistic health practitioner, transformational life coach, speaker, and author.

Her areas of interest include energy medicine, inner alchemy, and spiritual awareness.

Embracing the belief that life is an expression of the choices we make, she's a teacher and student of purposeful living.

With tremendous respect for the earth's natural resources, Laurie's goal is to leave the slightest footprint on the planet while making a lasting impression on its inhabitants: one that's positive, uplifting, constructive, and healing.

A cross between Dr. Dolittle, Nanny McPhee, and a Type-A Buddhist, she's an active listener, observer of details, payer of attention, reader and writer of books, unabashed optimist, and kindness enthusiast.

She enjoys yoga, long walks, bicycling, and photographing the great outdoors. She loves laughter, red licorice, and all things Idaho.

A minimalist by intent, she lives a beautiful life with fewer things—simple, yet full.

Laurie Buchanan's previous book, *Note to Self: A Seven-Step Path to Gratitude and Growth,* is a 2016 Idaho Author Award winner for inspiration, 2016 Foreword INDIES Book of the Year gold winner, 2017 International Excellence Body, Mind, Spirit Book Awards finalist, 2016 Nautilus silver award winner, and 2017 International Book Awards gold winner.

"Don't go with the flow, or against it. Create your own."

—**LAURIE BUCHANAN,** holistic health practitioner, transformational life coach, and author

Author photo © Len Buchanan